ACADIAN EXILES
in the
GOLDEN COAST
of
LOUISIANA

Sidney A. Marchand
COPYRIGHT, 1943, BY SIDNEY A. MARCHAND, DONALDSONVILLE, LOUISIANA.

THE GOLDEN COAST OF LOUISIANA

Ascension and Saint James Parishes

The First Acadian Settlement:

Saint James Parish.

The Second Acadian Settlement:

Ascension Parish, in Louisiana

Where the exiles, by the Grace of God, found peace, security and happiness.

———

Pax Domini sit semper vobiscum.

TO MY GRANDPARENTS

Joseph Alexandre Marchand...... (1836-1867)

Madeleine Octavie Landry .... (1841-1862)

Hiram H. Carver .... (1829-1903)

Emma Bourg .... (1840-1884)

"To-day, as well as in the future, may a
Louisianian and a Frenchman never meet without feeling
that they are bound by the tenderest ties of fraternal affection and may they always refer to one another as brothers;
. . . may they act as brothers in their joint labors for the
greater good and welfare of humanity at large."

—Pierre Clement de Laussat, Nov. 30, 1803.

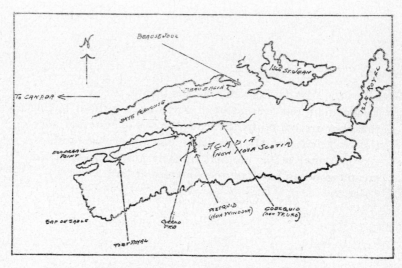

Old Acadia, now Nova Scotia, scene of the expulsion of 1755.

Contents

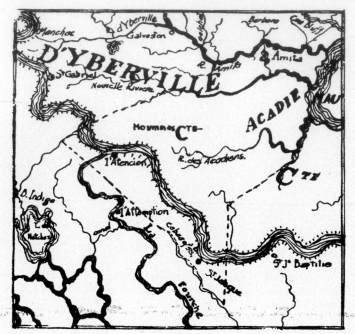

The county of Acadia, Louisiana, now St. James and Ascension parishes, known as the "Golden Coast."

"They were approaching the region where reigns perpetual summer,
Where through the Golden Coast
Sweeps with majestic curve the river away to the eastward."

—*Longfellow.*

INTRODUCTION

"They settled above the German coast, on both sides of the Mississippi, and in the course of time their plantations connected the latter settlement with that of Baton Rouge and Pointe Coupee. It is, at this day, known by the appellation of the Acadian coast."

Martin, *"History of Louisiana,"* p. 188.

THE statement of an eminent historian to the effect that "A lively desire of knowing and of recording our ancestors so generally prevails, that it must depend upon the influence of some common principle in the minds of men," is probably concurred in by all members of the human family. "We seem to have lived in the persons of our forefathers," asserts the same writer. All of us love to meditate on their day and time, commune with them in spirit, re-create mental pictures of their homes, farms and families, and, in general, participate in their joys and sorrows and their tears and laughter.

To illustrate my point, let us imagine that we reside in the ecclesiastical parish known as "Ascension," in the district of Lafourche des Chetimaches, and that the date is the fifth day of October, in the year of Our Lord One Thousand Seven Hundred and Eighty. It has been announced that the authorities of the Church of Ascension, now Ascension Catholic church, have decided to dispose of the upper portion of the church land. We attend High Mass, and we find that almost everyone is present, and that nearly all are Acadian exiles. No other church is found in all Ascension parish. When the solemn services are concluded, the Spanish commandant, Louis Judice, proceeds to the front door of the church and with due solemnity offers the land for sale to the last and highest bidder. Commandant Judice has already offered the land for sale on the two preceding Sundays, making a genuine effort to secure the best bidder. All public sales are held at the front door of the church. On this particular Sabbath the tract which he is to sell has a frontage on the Mississippi river of three arpents with a depth of forty arpents. No improvements whatsoever are situated thereon, and the land is covered with woods and underbrush, and without any fencing. Father Reuillogodos has valued the tract—one hundred twenty arpents—at $50.00. Commandant Judice has exerted every effort to get a good price for the land, and after "crying in a loud and audible voice," for a considerable period of time on three consecutive Sundays, the best bid obtainable was the offer of Etienne Landry who bid $242.00. The land was adjudicated to Landry as being "the last, best and highest bidder." Thus, we find that on October 5, 1780, land in the heart of the present city of Donaldsonville, Louisiana, was purchased at the price of $2.00 per arpent. (CB C, fo. 383).

The first and second Acadian settlements (St. James and Ascension parishes, Louisiana, respectively) were originally settled by groups of dejected, disconsolate and mistreated Acadian exiles who had been banished from Acadia (now Nova Scotia) in 1755. Following their expulsion they were transported to various sections of the world, but principally to the eastern portion of what is now our United States of America, and were scattered along the Atlantic coast from Massachusetts to Georgia. Those who were cast ashore in Maryland and further south longed to reach French New Orleans and Spanish Louisiana.

Writers without number have told and retold the sad, tragic and stirring story of the burning of Grand Pre, and the events which preceded and followed the destruction of the village, and the writer will not attempt to again relate or discuss the alleged reasons and causes leading to the expulsion of the Acadians, or the circumstances surrounding it, except in a very general way. Instead, the writer will try to "find" the exiles in the Golden Coast of Louisiana, "see" their settlements and note their progress. Let us follow them from Grand Pre, Piziquid and Beaubasin to the Golden coast! The Le Blancs, Landrys, Melancons, Brauds, Babins, Boudreauxs, Heberts, Dugas, Bourgeois and Gautreaus!

In the years which followed 1755—the year of the expulsion—numerous groups of Acadians, overcoming the obstacles which usually confront all pioneers, made their way to New Orleans, and thence, in due time, "up the river" to the First and Second Acadian settlements. In this fertile region they were assigned to the wild and uninhabited lands which bordered on the Father of Waters. Whether it was May or December made little difference, as the climate was very mild and the scenery beautiful. On the wooded lands allotted to them, they made little "clearings," felling the trees, and enlarging the cultivable lands by means of additional "deadenings" each year. Hereon they erected rude cabins, without floors, with posts in the ground, covered with split boards and surrounded with pickets. And within these humble homes dwelt a free, peaceful and religious people.

Who were the exiles who settled in the First and Second Acadian settlements? Where were their farms located? What of their homes? Their families? Their church? The writer has imposed upon himself the task of re-assembling them into family groups, of relocating their farms, of reconstructing their simple homes of posts, pickets, boards and dirt floors, but, by reason of the terrific world conflict now raging, the publication of the manuscript relating to the family groups has been "indefinitely postponed."

14

Available church and public records are necessarily old, faded and written in Latin, Spanish and French. Fortunately, my good friends and pastors, Fathers C. M. Chambon and Raphael C. Labit, of Ascension Catholic church, and Hon. James S. Barman, chief-deputy clerk of court, generously accorded to the writer every courtesy possible in order to make the ancient records available for examination and scrutiny. I extend to them my deep appreciation and thanks. I also take this opportunity to thank former Mayor Henry Arthur Folse, Mayor George Richard Blum, J. Clarence Bouchereau, John H. Schaff, Bertin Duplessis, Sybil Landry, Anna Mae Alonzo, B. C. Alwes, Henry A. Dugas, clerk of court, Lester Gonzales, sheriff, and A. C. Simoneaux, president of the police jury, Louis L. Blanc, chief of police, and all others who have assisted me in this undertaking.

All "eye-witnesses" to the stirring events of the pioneer days in the first and second Acadian settlements, having long ago become a part and parcel of the hallowed soil where they pitched "their tents" as exiles, the entire story, picture and history must be drawn, reconstructed and re-created from written records.

Originally it was the writer's intention to confine this work to the Acadian exiles exclusively, but it was later decided to include all settlers of this region who established themselves hereabout prior to 1800. It is regrettable that a work of this kind was not written about the years 1810 or 1825, while some of the exiles were still living, and when they in person could have given first-hand testimony of their experiences. The exiles were in truth and in fact the founders and builders of the "Golden Coast of Louisiana," and are worthy of every tribute paid them herein.

When William Donaldson, in 1806, established his "Donaldson Town," he named a street "Acadia," in memory of the birthplace of the exiles, but ungrateful time has obliterated even this little tribute. To-day, not a street or avenue in the city of Donaldsonville—settled by Acadian exiles—bears a name or title in memory of

"The Acadian land on the shores of the Basin of Minas."

SIDNEY A. MARCHAND.

Donaldsonville, Louisiana, U. S. A.,
May 1, 1943.

France Takes Possession of Louisiana

ONE hundred ninety years elapsed between the day of the discovery of the New World by Columbus—October 12, 1492—and the time of the ascent or descent of the great Mississippi river throughout its length by any European. We find that as late as the year 1700 very little was known of the location, characteristics, extent or topography of either ancient or modern Louisiana. The great Mississippi valley, with its millions of fertile acres, was almost unknown to the European, notwithstanding the fact that more than two centuries had passed since 1492. From time immemorial the Chetimaches, Houmas and Bayou Goulas Indians had roamed along the banks of the Father of Waters in what is now southern Louisiana. Their origin and the date of their arrival is lost in obscurity. All details are hidden in the fathomless past.

We next find Robert Cavalier de La Salle, foremost explorer of his day, in the spring of the year 1682, departing from Fort Creve Coeur (now near Peoria, Ill.) in his attempt to discover "the end" of the river Colbert or Mississippi. He was accompanied by twenty-two fellow Frenchmen and twenty-eight Indians—all brave adventurers who were ready and prepared to face all obstacles and dangers in order to raise the flag of France in new lands. Onward and onward, day after day and night after night, the little band floated down the mighty river, determined to explore the stream to is fullest extent. On March 15, 1682, they reached the Arkansas village, rested there, and then proceeded southward. It is safe to assume that this never-to-be-forgotten band of explorers paddled their pirogues, canoes and dug-outs through what is now Ascension and St. James parishes, Louisiana, during the latter part of March or the early part of April, in the year 1682. We may imagine what looks of surprise, consternation and defiance were written upon the brows of our predecessors—the Chetimaches, Houmas and Bayou Goula Indians—at beholding the intruders.

April 9th, 1682 was indeed a great day for La Salle and his companions, for on that day and date they actually reached "the end of the river" near the Gulf of Mexico. La Salle offered thanks to the Almighty for having guided him, and erected a huge wooden cross on the banks of the Colbert or Mississippi river. He proclaimed in a loud voice:

"For and on behalf of the all mighty, all powerful, invincible and victorious Prince, Louis the Great, by the grace of God, King of

16

France and Navarre, the fourteenth of that name. . . . I . . . have taken and do take possession . . . of the country known as Louisiana . . . upon the assurance given us by all these people that we are the first Europeans who have ascended or descended the full length of the Colbert river. . . ."

He further asserted and proclaimed that he had previously obtained the consent of the Chaouesnons, Chickasas, Otantatas, Isllinois, Matsigameas, Arkansas, Natchez and Koroas Indians, "who are the most important nations or tribes living in that section of the country, with whom we have signed treaties . . ." This statement prompts the writer to ask the question whether the Indians understood that they thereby divested themselves of all title to the soil, and thereby transferred it to a European power? More than a century afterwards, the supreme court of Louisiana so decided. (See 5 Mart. OS 655; 4 Ann. 141; 6 Rob. 175).

The photographer was unknown and the artist did not accompany the expedition, therefore, posterity must use its powers of imagination to picture and behold the awe-inspiring scenes of grandeur which greeted the eyes of the voyageurs as they rounded every bend of the majestic river, as it madly rushed for the open sea. Forests and more forests—rare, beautiful and untouched by the hand of man. Mile after mile, throughout their journey of over a thousand miles, La Salle and his men beheld amazing sights. Now and then they passed some Indian village; some were large while others were small, but all were potential "danger spots" to La Salle and his men. No levees or embankments obstructed the vision of the travelers in their view of the forests, and, history records, that the forests abounded with wild life and the river "teemed" with alligators.

La Salle had just cause to be proud of his accomplishments, and looked forward to greater deeds of discovery. Fate, however, decreed otherwise, for on March 19, 1687—less than five years after he placed the Cross at the southern end of the river—he was slain by one of his own men.

Twelve years subsequent to the death of La Salle we note that the French have established a settlement at Biloxi, with Iberville and Bienville in charge. It, therefore, devolved upon them to prosecute further the claims of France, and to settle and develop the lands explored and claimed by La Salle. Thus, we find Iberville and Bienville departing from Biloxi in February, 1699, to make a more detailed inspection and examination of the lower Colbert or Mississippi river regions. Shortly thereafter, as they ascended the river, they met a party of Washitas at the fork of the Chetimaches—that is, at the fork in the river Colbert or Mississippi in the land of the Chetimaches Indians. For more than a century thereafter the junction of the Bayou Lafourche and the Mississippi river (now Donaldsonville, Louisiana) was known and referred to as "La fourche des Chetimaches."

17

Notwithstanding the statement of the immortal La Salle that he took possession of Louisiana by and with the consent and acquiescence of the principal nations of tribes of Indians, we find that the Red man bitterly resented this instrusion (as he construed it) by the white man of his ancient domain. Had not he and his forefathers held this portion of mother earth from time immemorial? Thus, he reasoned, no mortal has the right to disturb him or evict him. The Chetimaches Indians dwelt in villages in and about what is now the Bayou Lafourche country. They were not numerous and were probably scattered. It appears that they were among those who were not satisfied at this encroachment by the white man. (5 Mart. OS 490). Missionary priests of the Roman Catholic church had accompanied La Salle on his journey of exploration of 1682, and other misionaries followed from year to year. One of these servants of the Prince of Peace became a martyr to the cause in December, 1704. Father John Buisson de St. Cosme, while engaged in his religious work, tied his pirogue to the bank of the Mississippi river near the present site of Donaldsonville, Louisiana. During the night, while he and his companions slumbered, they were murdered by the Chetimaches. On hearing the news of the death of the daring missionary priest, Governor Bienville was outraged, and he "sent presents to his (Indian) allies on the Mississippi, to induce them to declare war against these (Chetimaches) Indians. He was not able to raise more than eighty warriors." Martin, "History of Louisiana," p. 110. See, also, "The Story of Ascension parish, Louisiana," p. 10.

The campaign of extermination opened by Governor Bienville continued relentlessly until the year 1719. Under the terms of the treaty of peace, the Chetimaches were required to remove themselves and all their holdings to Bayou Jacques, now Bayou Jacob, near Plaquemine, La. It is said that when peace was finally declared, the Indian chief expressed his joy, in part, as follows:

"How beautiful is the sun to-day, in comparison with what it was when thou wert angry with us! How dangerous is one villain! Thou knowest that a single man has killed the chief of prayer, whose death has caused that of our best warriors: we have only old men and women, with their children, remaining, who all stretch out their arms to thee as to a good father. The gall that formerly filled thy heart, has given way to honey; the Great Spirit is no longer irritated against our nation; thou has required the head of a villain from our hands, and in order to obtain peace we have sent it to thee."

About this time Governor Bienville decided that the territorial capital should be located on the Mississippi river, instead of at Biloxi. After consultation with Indian advisors and scouts, he selected the spot where old New Orleans—Vieux Carre—now stands. That spot bounded by Canal and North Rampart streets, Esplanade avenue and the Mississippi river was subdivided into squares and lots, and the

18

infant village of New Orleans was presented to the world in the year 1717. Only five years thereafter—in 1822—Bienville transferred the French colonial capital from Biloxi to what is now "America's most interesting city."

Thus, in the land descriptions in a great many of the deeds to the early settlers, we find that the land is situated so many miles above "le capital."

FRENCH SETTLERS WHO PRECEDED THE ACADIANS

IT APPEARS reasonably certain that very few land grants were made by the French government to settlers in what is now Ascension and St. James parishes, Louisiana, prior to the arrival of the Acadian exiles. The writer has been unable to locate any such grants, or to find anything definite on this particular phase of the history of the "Golden Coast." Judge F. X. Martin, eminent historian and jurist, states that in the early part of the eighteenth century several large grants of land were made by the French government, and that among them was a certain grant to Marquis d'Anconis at the Houmas.[1] Local histories seem to be barren of any further reference to the d'Anconis grant. Judge Martin further states that sixty men arrived in April, 1718, to occupy the land which had been granted to Paris Duvernay, opposite Bayou Manchac.[2] The mere fact that the village of New Orleans in 1722 contained, as Judge Martin states, "one hundred cabins, placed without much order, a large wooden warehouse, two or three dwelling houses," would indicate that very few permanent settlers were established on the river Colbert or Mississippi eighty miles above that village, hamlet or outpost. The same historian mentions, however, the friction which existed between the Chetimaches Indians and some of the early settlers.

The archives of the office of the recorder of the parish of Ascension, Louisiana, contain a very few deeds and contracts dated as early as 1768, 1769, 1770 and 1771. Louis Judice, who was appointed "Commandant of the Acadians," maintained his office at Kabahanosse (now the village of St. James, La.), and removed his official residence to the present site of Donaldsonville, Louisiana, in the latter part of 1771 or January, 1772, for on the latter date we find him using the title "Commandant and Judge at Lafourche des Chetimaches."

A chapel, or building where religious services were held, was in existence at Lafourche des Chetimaches (now Donaldsonville, La.) prior to August 15, 1772, but on that date Father Angelus Reuillogodos established his residence here, and became the first resident priest of Ascension Catholic church.

In view of the foregoing, it is the opinion of the writer that very few, if any, permanent settlers were established in what is now Ascension and St. James parishes, Louisiana, prior to the arrival of the first contingent of Acadian exiles.

---

1 Martin, "History of Louisiana," p. 127.
2 Opposite Plaquemine point, Iberville parish, La.

Expulsion of the Acadians—Farewell to Grand Pre

THE earliest records of the recorder's office of the parish of Ascension, Louisiana, disclose that all of the original settlers of the second Acadian settlement—Ascension parish—were exiles from Acadia and the surrounding country. These records further show that a considerable proportion of these settlers came from Piziquid, now Windsor, a village or settlement about fifteen miles from Grand Pre. Others departed from homes at Grand Pre, now Wolfville, Cobequid, now Truro, Beaubassin or Bourgeois settlement, Riviere aux Canards, Beausejour (now Fort Cumberland), Port Royal, now Annapolis Royal), and various other points throughout the countryside of "old Acadie," now Nova Scotia.

The story of the expulsion of the Acadians from the Maritime provinces of Canada—Acadia and the adjacent islands—has been told again and again, and we shall not endeavor to add or detract from anything that has already been said in reference to that tragic and heartrending occurrence. Let us, however, touch upon the principal events of this drastic plan of the British to eliminate, eradicate and exterminate all opposition to their government throughout Canada and Acadia.

It is related that when the war between the English and French began in 1755, the Acadians were deeply sympathetic towards the cause of the French. They were legally supposed to remain neutral. However, when the British captured Fort Beausejour they were astonished to find a considerable number of armed Acadians therein. Thereupon, the British evolved the plan of expulsion, whereby all the Acadians would be scattered abroad on the seven seas, and their farms and homes destroyed, so that none would return.

The master-minds set about to formulate a plan of action, and it was decided that the best plan was to trap the Acadians in their house of worship. The holy altar, therefore, was about to witness this unusual and novel procedure. Commander John Winslow was commissioned to be the executioner. On September 4, 1755 he issued the following summons to the humble farmers and fishermen of Grand Pre and the surrounding territory:

"To the inhabitants of the district of Grand Pre, Riviere des Mines, Riviere aux Canards, and adjacent thereto.

". . . His Excellency has instructed us concerning his recent decision . . .

21

"Consequently, I order and strictly enjoin by these presents to all the inhabitants of the above named districts and all other districts, aged and young men and boys of ten years upward to appear at the church of Grand Pre, on Friday, the 5th instant, at three o'clock in the afternoon, in order that we may cause them to be made aware of the instructions which we have been ordered to communicate to them. I declare that no excuse, under any pretext, will be admitted, and this, under penalty of confiscation of their property and effects in default of other fortune.

"Given at Grand Pre, September 2d (4th?) in the 29th year of the reign of His Majesty, A. D. 1755."

In obedience to this proclamation or summons, a large number—418 of the fathers of families and principal inhabitants—presented themselves in the church of St. Charles at Grand Pre. All their lives they had prayed daily in this church and before its altar. It was to them a place of refuge and of consolation in their sorrows. When inside the structure on Friday, September 5, 1755, and while awaiting pronouncement of the promised message, the doors were closed, and soldiers took charge. Commander Winslow then read aloud the following proclamation:

"Gentlemen: I have received from His Excellency, Governor Lawrence (of Massachusetts), the instructions of the King which I hold in my hands. It is by these orders I have convened you to receive the final decision of His Majesty regarding French inhabitants of the province of Nova Scotia where, for more than half a century, you have been the beneficiaries of this great indulgence. . . .

"I, therefore, communicate to you, without hesitation, the orders and instructions of His Majesty, as follows: That all your lands and houses, beasts of all kinds and cattle of every nature, are confiscated by the Crown, also all of your other property, save your money and movables, and that you yourselves will be removed from this province." (See Lauvriere, v. 1, p. 464).

The message fell like a thunder-bolt upon the assembly. They were in church, unarmed and unprepared in any way to offer resistance, and, in fact, under the guns of the British. Remonstrations were vain and useless. The Acadians had left families at home who expected them to return in a few hours. A few of the prisoners were sent out to notify all others to report immediately for "arrest."

Through the courtesy of Senator Dudley J. Le Blanc, of Lafayette, Louisiana, a descendant of the exiles, the writer is permitted to use the following list of names of those who were imprisoned at Grand Pre in 1755, the original spelling being retained, to-wit:

Pierre Alin	Ettimme Boudro	Charls Robs Choct
Jean Apigne	Charle Boudo	Jean Robs Choc

Oliver Aucoin
Claud Ancoine
Charles Ancoine
jean Ancoine
Renez Ancoine
Joseph Ancoine
Alexandre Ancoine
jean Batiste Ancoine
Charles Ancoine
Pierre Ancoine
Simon Ancoine
Abraham Ancoine

Simon Ancoine
Charles Ancoine
Martin Ancoine
Oliver Ancoine
jean a Pierre Ancoine
Charles Ancoine

Aman Baben
Simon Babin
Johanes Babbin
Joseph Babin
Battistes Babin
Pierre Babin
Joseph Babin
Jean Babin
Paul Babin
Joseph Babin
Simon Babin
Jos. Babin
Rener Babin
feler Babin
Charls Babin
Joseph Babin

Jacques Bellemere
joseph Belmere
Renez Belmere

Oliver Belfontaine

Oliver Belfountain
Francois Benois
Joseph Benois
Joseph Blanchard
Aman Blanchard
Pierre ilasis Blana
pierre Bobin
Josep Boudro sits

Marin Boudro
Paul Boudro
Jean Boudro
Jeseyah Boudro
Jean Laris Boudro
jean Battiste Boudro
Charle Boudro
Pierre Boudro
Claude Boudro
Anselme Boudro
pierrs Boudro
paul Boudro

Josepj Boudro
pierrs Boudro
Paul Boudro
Joseph Boudro
joseph Boudro
Pierre Boudro
Norez Michael Boudro

Benons Bourg
le Vieux Rener Bouns
Michel Bourgh
Francis Bouer

Joseph Brassin
Cherussim Braux
Commo Brasseux
Charles Brans
Pierrs Brane
Vicar francis braux
Paul Brune
Joseph Brune
Pierre Brune
Aman Brune
Joseph Brune

Paul Capierre
Pierre Caretter

Antoine Celestine

Joseph Celestin
Paul Celestine
Norez Celestine
Charle Celestine
Pierre Celestine
Jacques Celve

Jacques Cleland

Clotis ————
finmi Chelle
Pierre Commo
"le Vieux Commo"
Joseph Commo
Vestache Commo
jean Battiste Commo
Eteeme Commo
Alexis Commo
Oliver Commo
Pierre Commo
Simon Commo

Norez Commo
Bassil Commo
Domique Cotoe

Jean Baptiste Daigree
jean Baxirles Daigree
Charle Daigre
Norez Daigre
Oliver Daigre fils
Oliver Daigle
Brenar Daigre
Joseph Daigre
Astaches Daigre
Battistes Daigre
Alin Daigre
Charls Daigre
pierrs Daigre
Norez Daigre

jean Battiste David

Joseph Doiron
Pierre Boulet
jean Doucet
jean doulet

Alexandre Duon
Joseph dupuis
Jean Dupuis

Fabien Duquis
Silven Duquis
Simon Duquis
Germain Duquis
jean batiste Duquis
Aman Duquis
Antoine Duquis
Francois Duquis

Joseph Boudro
Pierre Boudro
Abraham Boudro
Michel Boudro
Michel Boudro fils
Antoine Duzoy

Tunislaps Forrest
Oliver Forest

Josses inferms
habitant in firmis

Charles Jean sonne
Joseph Gotro
Charle Gotro
Alexxis Gotro
jean Gitro
pierrs gautro
paul Gotro
Charle Gotror
jean gotro

Joseph Gotro
Alexis gotro
Paul Gotro
Aman Gotro

pierre a gouitin

Pierre Gronger
jean Battis Granger

jean Granger
Sorans Granger
Simon Granger
Charles Granger
Joseph Granger
Rener Granger
Charle Granger
Francois Granger
Jean Granger
Joseph Granger
msemine Granger
Joseph Granger

Franciss Granger
Charle Granger
Aman Granger
Joseph Granger
Aman Granger

Pierre Clemenson
Lewis Pierre Cloatre
George Cloatre

joseph Robs Chard
francois hebert
paul hebert
pierre hebert
francois hebert
francois hebert
Alexandre Hebert
Aman Hebert

jos. hebert
Bennos hebert
Guilljaums Hebert
Benonis hebert
joseph hebert
Simon hebert
Alexis hebert
charle hebert

Charle Jean sonne

Alexandre Landry
Pierre Landry
jean a Pierre Landry
Charle Landry
Antoine Landry apsen
jeanmer Landry
Alexxis Landry
Charle Landry
Antoine Landry
Germain Landry
jean Landry
Renez Landry
jean Landry fil
Paul Landry
Jos. Landry
Aman Landry
Fromer Landry
jean Landry
Francois Landry
Paul Landry

jos. Landry
Charle Landry
Pierre Landry
Jose Landry
Charle Landry

jean Duquis
Alexandr Duquis
Michell Duquis
Suprian Dupiers
Charle Dupier
Auguste Le Blanc
Baptiste Le Blanc
Simon Le Blanc
Paul Le Blanc
Jean Le Blanc
Francois Le Blanc
Francois Le Blanc
  Tus
Pierre Le Blanc
Renez Le Blanc
Pierre La Blanc
Jean Battiste Le Blanc
Benois Le Blanc
Charle Le Blanc
Jacques La Blanc
Simon Le Blanc
Pierre Le Blanc

Oliver Le Blanc
Charle Le Blanc
Joseph Le Blanc
Charle Le Blanc
Marin Le Blanc
Joseph Le Blanc
Joseph Le Blanc
Oliver Le Blanc
Joseph Le Blanc
Jean Charle Le Blanc
Michelle Le Blanc
Blesse Le Blanc
Simon Le Blanc
Bonaumturs Le Blanc
Jean Le Bland
Francois Le Blanc
Battistes La Blanc
Daniell Le Blanc
Alin Le Blanc
Joseph Le Blanc
Simon Le Blanc
Joseph Le Blanc du
  sour
Maturin Le Blanc
pierrs Le Blanc
Charls Le Blanc Cems
paul Le Blanc
jem pierrs le Blens

24

Germain Duquis
Joseph Hebert

Pierre Hebert
Joseph Hebert
Manuel Hebert
Pierre Hebert
Oliver Hebert
jean Hebert
Joseph Hebert
Norez Hebert
Etimme Hebert
Pierre Hebert
Augustin Herbert
Renez Hebert
Aman Hebert
jacques Hebert
Oliver Hebert
Augustin
Joseph Hebert
Charle Hebert
Antaine Hebert
jgneiff Hebert
Pierre Hebert
Simon Pierre Hebert
Germain hebert
jean Battistes hebear
Paul heberr
Paul Melanson
Baptistes Mellanson

Alexandre Melanson
Pierre Jane Melanson
Battiste Melanson
Jean Battis Melanson
Joseph Melanson
Pierre Melanson
James Melanson
Pierre Jean Melanson
Aman Melanson
Pierre Melanson
Jacques Melanson
Joseph Muiller
Anselmer ales Mengean

Pierre Noalis

Antoine Pitree
Dominique Pitre
Simon Pitre
Simon Pitre

Germain Landry
Battiste Landry

Etimme Landry
Etair Landry
Simon Landry
Jean Landry
Michelle Landry
Michalle Landry
Martin Landry
Jean Landry
Germain Landry
Rener Landry
Charls Landry
Rener Landry
Pierrs Landry
le petis Clauds Landry
Etime Landry

Pierre LeClane
Pierre Le Blanc
Pierre jean LeBlanc
Norez Le Blanc
Jean Baptiste LeBlanc
Michelle Le Blanc
Pierre LeBlanc
Charle Lablun
Pinions Le Blanc
Joseph Richard
Jean Richard

Jean Richard
Jaque Richard
Pierre Richard
Jos. Richard
Charles Richard
Paul Richard
Paul Richard

Francis Rous

Baptiste Sapin
James Sapin
Joseph Semer
Charle Sonier
Pierre Sosonier
Renez Sosonier
Machalle Sorere
Marelle Soner

Pierre Terriot

Joseph Le Blanc
Jean jos le Blens

Simon Le Blanc
Bernard Le Blanc
jacques Le Blanc
pierrs La Blanc
jean jauque Le Blanc
Oliver Le Blanc
Allin Le Blanc
Joseph Le Blanc

Felix Laurent
Paul Lebar
jean Lebare
Norez Lebare
Margaret Lapierre
Delenne Leuron
Jean LaPrince
Joseph labous
Brunos le gronger
jean le Sour

Antoine Majet
Jean Baptiste Masier
Battis Massier
Amans Massier
Battistes Massier
Pierre Terriote
Jean Teriot

Charles Teriot
Jacque Teriot
Brunois Terriote
Charles Tibodo
Joseph Tibodo
Paul Tibodo
Germain Tibodo
Joseph Trahase
Pierre Trahan
Claude Trahan
Michelle Trahan
Charles Trahan
Charles Trahan
jean Trahan
Renez Trahan
Pierre Trahan
Joseph Trahan
Joseph Trahan
jean Trahan
Charles Trahan

	janis Terriot	jean Batistes Trahan
Bour quette	Charles a Claude Terriot	Pierre Trahan
Michelle Richard	Suprien Terriot	Joseph Trahan
Basil Richard	Charle Terriot	
Renez Richard	Germain Terriot	Charle Tunour
Germain Richard	Pierre Terriote	Joseph Vincent
Joseph Richard	Oliver Terriot	Antoine Vincent

A booklet published by the government of Nova Scotia reports the "The number collected for removal from Grand Pre was 1,923 souls." Lauvriere (v. 1, p. 264) thinks that a total of 7,000 Acadians were banished from their homeland, as follows: 1,100 from Beaubassin, 1,600 from Grand Pre, 1,100 from Piziquid, 582 from Minas, 1,664 from Port Royal, and several hundred from Halifax.

Driven aboard transports without being told of their destinations they were scattered about all up and down the Atlantic coast. The British claim that every effort was made to keep families together, but in spite of this many families were separated, some of them never to meet again.

"Tomb of an Acadian exile, who was born at Baltimore. The inscription on the tombstone being: Simon Sylvain LeBlanc, ne a Baltimore, Etats Unis d'Amerique, le 5 Novembre 1765." Catholic cemetery, Donaldsonville, La.

26

New River Lane

Ruins of home built by Acadian exile, showing the mixture of mud and moss used in the walls. Chief of Police, Louis L. LeBlanc, a descendant of the Acadian exile is shown in the foreground.

A HOMELESS PEOPLE WANDER—DREAM OF DISTANT LOUISIANA

"It is due to the descendants of the British colonists, to say that their sires received with humanity, kindness and hospitality those who so severely smarted under the calamities of war."

Martin, *"History of Louisiana,"* p. 187.

FROM the foregoing we have seen that the Acadians were scattered to the four-winds. Some were cast ashore in Massachusetts, New York, Virginia and Maryland; others were sent down south—to North Carolina, Georgia, while others were transported to England and other English colonies far away. Let us, in a general way, follow the exiles who ultimately found refuge in southern Louisiana, and particularly those who settled in what later became known as the "Golden Coast" —Ascension and St. James parishes, Louisiana.

It appears that as early as 1758 small groups of the exiles, who had been cast ashore in Georgia, the Carolinas and Maryland, arrived in Louisiana and settled on the banks of the Mississippi river above New Orleans. (Lauvriere, v. 2, p. 194). The writer does not think, however, that these established themselves on the Mississippi river as far up as the first or second Acadian settlements. Later, on Feb. 23, 1764, we dicover a group of 193 exiles who arrived in New Orleans from San Domingo; while on May 13th of the same year, 48 Acadian families followed. In April, 1765, still others followed, and were sent to the Attakapas region.

Judge Felix Voorhies, in his book, "Acadian Reminiscence," gives an interesting account of the journey of the exiles from Maryland to Louisiana, as related to him by his grandmother. The judge's grandmother was a member of the group of exiles who were dispatched to Maryland. After remaining with the hospitable strangers in Maryland for about three years,—during all of which time they yearned to reach Louisiana—they finally decided upon an overland journey to French territory on the lower Mississippi. After bididng a tearful adieu to the Smith and Brent families in Maryland, as Judge Voorhies relates, he proceeds to write the story as told him by his grandmother, as follows:

"We set out in a westerly direction . . . But we were lulled by the hope that far, far away in Lousiana, our dreamland, we would find our kith and kin. . . . As long as we journeyed in Virginia, . . . our progress, though slow, was satisfactory. The people were generous, and supplied us with an abundance of provisions." Onward they proceeded and found North Carolina to be a wild and mountainous country. After the expiration of two months on the road, they reached the Tennessee river, where the exiles met friendly Canadian hunters. These friends recommended, as the shortest route to Louisiana, that the exiles float down the Tennessee river out to the Mississippi, and thence down the latter to Louisiana. Trees were felled and a boat was built, and just as this journey was to begin a great loss was sustained—Rene Le Blanc, grand old man and leader of the expedition, was removed by the angel of death.

In due time, the Missisippi was reached, and the Acadians then became hopeful that the voyage would be crowned with success. Floating on the Father of Waters, day after day and night after night, a determined and brave band overcame all obstacles that confronted them. In due course, Bayou Plaquemine was reached, and entering this stream they struggled along until the Attakapas country—their land of Evangeline—was before them. The old grandmother, Judge Voorhies relates, liked the Attakapas country very much, but with tear-filled eyes, she mourned "I grieve for my native land—Acadia— with its rocks and snows, because I have left there a part of my heart in the graves of those I loved so well and who sleep under its sod." Indeed, "Acadian Reminiscences" is an interesting and instructive piece of Acadian lore.

The new arrivals were so numerous that the Spanish government considered it a veritable transformation of lower Louisiana into a new Acadia. Shortly after the beginning of the migration, the governor stated that there were then about three hundred exiles on the river coming to Louisiana to settle; that at least four thousand more would establish themselves here within a few years; that they were a brave, industrious and religious people, and are strongly attached to their prince and country. Ordonnateur Faucault observed that since the peace of 1762 the population of the colony had increased by one-third. It appears that it was not until 1764 that the exiles learned that by the secret treaty of Fontainebleu, dated November, 1762, the territory of Louisiana had been transferred to Spain.

Lauvriere (v. 2, p. 482) states that whether they came from France or Acadia, the English or French colonies, or elsewhere, the exiles arrived in southern Louisiana between 1758 and 1785 so poor, undernourished and discouraged that the generous concessions of lands which they received in beautiful Louisiana seemed to them a terrestrial paradise. Prof. J. Hanno Deiler, in his excellent book, "The Settlement of the German Coast of Louisiana," p. 42, says:

"During this year (1768) Ulloa had taken from the Germans of

29

the German coast provisions to the value of 1500 piastres to feed the Acadians, who had but recently come into the colony, and were not able yet to sustain themselves."

In a foot-note he adds: "On the 28th day of February, 1765, 230 persons, natives of Acadia, arrived in Louisiana . . . Foucault . . . sent them to Opelousas and the country of the Attakapas. On the 4th of May, 1765, 80 persons from Acadia arrived and went to Opelousas. On the 5th of May, 1765, 48 Acadian families arrived and were sent to Opelousas." And next is found the sturdy pioneers of the First and Second Acadian settlements, for Prof. Deiler states:

"On the 16th of November, 1766, 216 Acadians arrived from Halifax. They were sent to Cabahanoce, the present parish of St. James. These were the ones who received the provisions which the Spanish government took from the Germans on the German coast."

Lauvriere says that they came from Halifax on an English boat which they rented or chartered at their own expense, and, quoting Faucault, he says:

"We furnished them agricultural tools, . . . and, during the first year of their establishment, we distributed to them the same rations which are given to the colonial troops . . . These refugees were established on both banks of the river (Mississippi) as far as Baton Rouge, in a region called 'Acadian coast'." (Lauvriere, v. 2, p. 194).

When the Acadians learned that their new homeland had been transferred from France to Spain, they were very much disturbed. All resolved that they were ready to "sacrifice their property and their lives to remain always French." Aubry reported that if the country remained French the settlers would be overwhelmed with joy. The Acadian leaders appear to have been active in the so-called revolution of 1768, when Governor Ulloa was forcibly ejected from the colony. Governor O'Reilly, upon his arrival, took drastic action to punish all alleged offenders, and eighteen prominent citizens were executed or imprisoned as traitors. The general situation then prevailing was so unsatisfactory to some of the exiles that they abandoned their lands and homes and departed for San Domingo. (Lauvriere, v. 2, p. 196).

However, in spite of the foregoing, we find that in 1785 a large number of exiles arrived, and the greater portion established themselves at Lafourche des Chetimaches—now Ascension parish, Louisiana. (Martin, id. p. 244). Thus we find in the archives of the Ascension Catholic church, at Donaldsonville, La., for the years 1785-86-87-88 numerous births, marriages and deaths among the Acadians. There are many entries which record the marriages of couples from the "new Acadian settlement at Lafourche." Baptisms of infants numbered 35 in 1775, while in 1788 the number had increased to 62.

The exiles were very religious, and probably 100% were members of the Roman Catholic church. It is said by Lauvriere (v. 2, p. 141) that they never spoke of anything but the Mass and their king. Father

Maillard, who was detained by the English at Halifax, wrote the exiles near Boston, in 1761, that he longed to be with them; that he felt that they were present in spirit in church each Sunday; that he remembers them to all the faithful, and asked that he be remembered by them in their prayers.

In the year 1785 the population of Lafourche was 646, while at Galveston, on the Amite, dwelt 242 inhabitants. In 1788, the population had increased to 1164, including the settlement of Valenzuela. (Martin, Id. p. 251). Within three years the population of the First and Second Acadian settlements had increased 51%. (Martin, Id. p. 252). In 1792, New Orleans was the place of abode of less than six thousand inhabitants.

Lauvriere states (v. 2, p. 197) that "In 1779 was founded the Acadian parish of St. James Cabahanoce." It appears, however, that the First Acadian settlement—St. James parish—was established much earlier than 1779, for in 1766 we find Louis Judice styling himself "commandant of the Acadians" and performing his official duties at his office which he maintained at Cabahanoce or Kabahanosse—St. James parish. (Orig. Act, "Q", p. 723). It may be that the settlers at Kabahanosse in the year 1766 were not numerous, but it appears certain that a considerable number were there in 1772.

In this connection, let us note the comment of Dr. W. A. Read, in his "Louisiana-French," p. 78, as follows:

". . . The edict of exile was not issued against the Acadians until 1755; and that perhaps ten years passed before any Acadians settled in Louisiana." Dr. Read discusses the origin of the name "Kabahanoce," and supposes that Michel Cantrelle, first commandant of St. James parish, and the father-in-law of Louis Judice, applied the name to his plantation which is situated on the west bank of the Mississippi, opposite Convent, La. Cantrelle was the first judge of Acadia county under the American government.

Commandant Louis Judice, during the years 1767-68-69 continued to serve as "commandant of the Acadians" at Kabahanosse. In 1770 he became "captain of militia and judge of Lafourche des Chetimaches," but he continued to maintain his office and perform his duties at "Kabahanosse." This, in the writer's opinion, establishes the fact that a number of settlers had established themselves at the Second Acadian settlement Ascension parish, La. as early as 1770 They were probably not numerous, but there were enough to demand attention from the commandant. Thus, a new title is conferred upon Louis Judice by the Spanish governor—he is now "Judge of LaFourche des Chetimaches." Two years thereafter—on January 9, 1772—we find him using the title "commandant and judge of Lafourche des Chetimaches" and performing his duties at the last mentioned place— probably on the tract of land on the upper side of Bayou Lafourche, where the village of Port Barrow is now situated. This tract was

31

granted to him by the Spanish governor. The ecclesiastical parish of Ascension now had its first resident public official.

It is but reasonable to assume that as soon as a score of Acadian families established themselves at Lafourche des Chetimaches, their leaders undertook to provide a suitable place where the exiles might celebrate Mass. They erected a small chapel, probably of cypress boards, posts and pickets obtained from trees felled on the site. The chapel was first served by a missionary priest, probably Father Ange de Reuillagodos. As reasons for reaching this conclusion, the writer assigns the following facts: 1. Commandant Judice was named "Judge of Lafourche des Chetimaches" in 1770, showing that a certain number of the settlers had established themselves here; 2. On December 25, 1771, Commandant Judice sold the estate of Joseph Lincour at the front door of the parochial church of Assumption, which church was located at Lafourche des Chetimaches, and 3. When Father Reuillagodos died (December 16, 1784) the church records noted that he had served as pastor of this church for *fourteen* years. Thus, it appears that from 1770 to this date, continuously and uninterruptedly, services of the Roman Catholic church have been held in the Second Acadian settlement—Ascension parish—at or very near the spot where they are presently held.

The exiles who found refuge in the Second Acadian settlement were happy and contented in their new surroundings; and others, hearing of their good fortune, followed. We find that by August 15, 1772, historic Ascension Catholic church (at what later became Donaldsonville, La.) was established, with Father Reuillagodos as first resident pastor. He named his ecclesiastical parish the "parish of Ascension" and dedicated it to the ascension of Our Lord. Following 1772, Commandant Louis Judice performed all of his official acts at the "parish" of Ascension. Here, let us record in cold type a few words of praise for Father Ange de Reuillagodos, the soldier of Christ, and for Louis Judice, the pioneer soldier and servant of the King. History, of both, can render but one verdict, that they were faithful, efficient and patriotic servants of their fellowmen, whose entire lives were devoted to the betterment of the cruel lot of the Acadian exiles.

From 1766 to 1770, Louis Judice served as commandant of the Acadians and maintained his office at Kabahanosse (St. James parish), and from 1770 to 1798—twenty-eight years—he served as commandant of the Second Acadian settlement—Ascension parish. This service was continuous and without interruption. It appears that the last official act of this worthy servant was performed on September 16, 1797. He was probably an old man by this time; and he was succeeded by Evan Jones (founder of Evan Hall plantation, McCall, La.) We find Jones acting as commandant on January 6, 1798. He was succeeded by Don Rafael Croquer, a Spanish scholar, who appears to have served from 1799 to Nov. 18, 1803. All of Croquer's official acts are written in Spanish in a hand-writing somewhat difficult to read. Croquer was followed by that distinguished Acadian exile, Joseph Landry, ancestor of a large number of Landrys who now reside in and around Ascension parish. When Louisiana was purchased by the United States, Governor Claiborne sent Dr. John Watkins to interview various people in the country with a view towards appointing new commandants wherever the old ones were not available for re-appointment. Of Joseph Landry, Dr. Watkins declared in his report to Governor Claiborne in 1804:

> "This gentleman, altho born in Acadia, has resided many years in Louisiana, speaks the English and French languages, professes strong attachment to the Government of the United States, and possesses the unlimited confidence and affection of all the inhabitants of the District in which he lives."

On the recommendations of Dr. Watkins, Joseph Landry was appointed the first commandant, under the American government, at Lafourche des Chetimaches, now Ascension parish, Louisiana.

J. Norbert Landry, great-grandfather of the writer, a grandson of an Acadian exile, a justice of the peace at what is now Prairieville, La., about 1845.

The Landry Tomb, Catholic cemetery, Donaldsonville, La. erected to the memory of Joseph Landry, Senator, representative and first commandant under the American government.

France Transfers Louisiana to Spain

Ostensibly to compensate Spain for losses sustained by her in having allied herself with France in the latter's war with Britain, France on November 3, 1762, by a secret treaty, transferred to Spain all that vast territory of Louisiana situated west of the Mississippi river, together with the city of New Orleans and the so-called island on which it stands. All French territory east of the Mississippi had previously been ceded to England under the terms of the treaty of peace.

The motives and reasons for the transfer will not be discussed herein, other than to set forth an extract from a letter written by Louis XV, of France to the Spanish king, wherein the ruler of France stated:

"I wish with all my heart that Spain should not suffer from a war which Your Majesty's personal regard for me made him undertake. If New Orleans and Louisiana could be of use to Your Majesty to gain the restitution of Havana or compensate Spain for the cessions that she would give the British, I offer the possession to her, and I would esteem it a great happiness to me in particular if certain cessions on my part could show Your Majesty my gratitude and my desire that the two crowns, according to the family compact, should make but a single body . . ."[3]

The cession of November 3, 1763 was not known to the Louisianians until 1764. This information was a terrific blow to the French and Acadian settlers. Louis XV and Charles III were apparently satisfied, but with the settlers it was different. Their love for France could not be transferred and traded by the mere signing on the dotted line. Sixty-four years had elapsed since the founding of Biloxi; almost forty

---

[3] An interesting discussion of this matter is found in La. Hist. Qy., vol. 19, No. 1, p. 204 and vol. 15, No. 2, p. 181. In the case of Newcombe v. Skipwith, 1 Mart. OS 151, the La. Supreme Court stated: "That France occupied the country on both sides of the river from the year 1698, when she began her establishments at Biloxi, under the name of Louisiana, 'till the 3rd of November, 1762, when by a secret treaty the island on which stands the city of New Orleans and her (France's) possessions on the western bank of the Mississippi, were ceded to Spain. It is true almost seven years elapsed before the Spanish took possession, but during that interval, since the Court of France put no obstacles to the possession of the country" the possession of France was possession by Spain.

years had elapsed since the transfer of the French capital from Biloxi to New Orleans, and eight tragic years had passed since the burning of Grand Pre.

Greatly agitated, the settlers threatened rebellion. Ulloa, the first Spanish governor, arrived in July, 1765, but owing to great opposition, did not enter New Orleans until March 5, 1766. He was displeased at the attitude taken by the settlers, and they were indignant that he should refuse to exhibit his credentials. Ulloa, in an attempt at "appeasement,"[4] decided to operate by and through one Aubry, a representative of the French government. It did not work, and everyone seemed dissatisfied at the attempt of Spain to take over the colony. The crisis was reached on October 29, 1768, when Spanish Governor Ulloa was forcibly expelled from New Orleans by Frenchmen, Acadians and German settlers. The settlers sat back and relaxed in the firm conviction that Spain would yield to the wishes of the inhabitants, and probably return the colony to France. However, the unexpected always happens.

The Spanish King became highly offended and indignant at the treatment accorded Governor Ulloa. He became determined to put down the so-called "rebellion." A strong man was needed. He scanned his list of availables and picked Alexander O'Reilly, to whom historians have applied the title "Bloody O'Reilly." This official, the second Spanish governor of Louisiana believed in "preparedness." He arrived at the Balize, at the mouth of the Mississippi, with a large number of soldiers, vessels, munitions, and accessories of war. Upon hearing of this, the leaders of the opposition to Spanish rule became alarmed and panicky. They realized that they could not wage war upon O'Reilly. On August 18, 1769 Alexander O'Reilly took actual possession of the territory of Louisiana. His proclamation made our forefathers subjects of Charles III. No longer were they Frenchmen. The leaders of the opposition were speedily tried, convicted and executed. History proclaims them patriots and lovers of liberty. Let us spread their names upon this page in tribute to the supreme sacrifice which they made. They are: Nicholas Chauvin de Lafraniere, Jean Baptiste Noyan, Pierre Caresse, Pierre Marquis and Joseph Millet.

Spanish domination being now an accomplished fact, the settlers made the best of it, though for years they nourished bitter resentment at the tyrannical methods of "Bloody O'Reilly." During all of this

---

4 Neville Chamberlain, we find, was not the first "appeaser."

period, small groups of Acadian exiles who had not reached this "Land of Evangeline" wandered from place to place, hoping, struggling and yearning to reach Louisiana. There they would meet fellow-Frenchmen who, upon beholding them, would greet them,

"Welcome once more, my friends, who so long have been friendless and homeless; Welcome once more to a home, that is better perchance than the old one!"

In his "History of Louisiana," p. 188, Judge Francois Xavier Martin describes the truly Christian welcome which the exiles were accorded in the then town of New Orleans, as follows:

"Like these, the Acadians were greeted with tenderness and hospitality; every house in the city afforded a shelter to some of these unfortunate people. Charity burst open the door of the cloister and the nuns ministered with profusion cheerfulness to the wants of the unprotected of their sex."

Ashland, colonial home of Duncan F. Kenner.

The First Acadian Settlement—St. James Parish, Louisiana

Jefferson College, Convent, La., the oldest educational institution in the First Acadian settlement. Now used as Manresa Retreat House.

NEW ORLEANS was established by Bienville in 1717, became the capital of colonial Louisiana in 1722, and, in 1769, was the home of three thousand one hundred ninety inhabitants. Judge Martin, as has already been noted, stated that in 1722 the village consisted of one hundred cabins, a large wooden warehouse, two or three dwelling houses, and a store-house.[5] Early settlers continued to select available sites for settlement above New Orleans on both banks of the Mississippi river. The German coast, now St. Charles and St. John parishes, was first settled. Thereafter, homeseekers proceeded onward and above these settlements, and in time established the First Acadian settlement, now St. James parish, and the Second Acadian settlement, now Ascension parish.

Having been expelled and banished from their homes in Acadia

---

[5] Martin, History of Louisiana, p. 147, also p. 168.

in 1775, and longing to join their brethren of the French race and to dwell again beneath the flag of that country, the Acadian exiles turned their eyes and hopes toward the fertile lands situated on both sides of the Mississippi river above the German settlements. The first contingent to arrive[6] was allotted lands above the German coast, thereby winning for their settlement the title "First" Acadian settlement. This is now the parish of St. James, and it appears to have been settled about 1763-1766. In October, 1763, some of the exiles who had managed to reach France, departed for Louisiana. A Mr. Aunier, one of the exiles, after reaching Louisiana, communicated with the "folks back home" and described conditions in such glowing terms, that immediately a large number of fellow-exiles in France decided to migrate to this land of plenty.[7]

Prof. J. Hanno Deiler, formerly of Tulane University, states that the first contingent of Acadians were sent to Cabahanose (St. James parish) on November 16, 1766. From the following he seems to be correct. On December 8, 1768, Governor Ulloa, writing concerning the so-called revolt, notes that the German settlers were greatly disappointed and dissatisfied at not having received settlement of their claim of 1,500 piastres for supplies furnished the Acadians. The Governor sent one Maxant to see about it, and the governor says:

"Maxant was arrested by Verret on the place of Cantrelle, the father-in-law of another Verret, and commander of the Acadians, where he was much maltreated."

Thus, it appears that Michel Cantrelle was appointed first commandant of the Acadians between November 4, 1766 and December 4, 1768. Prof. Deiler says further that by 1724 the settlers of the German coast "had already a chapel of their own." On page 65 he states "In 1771, the Germans of the upper German Coast built the church of St. John the Baptist in Edgard—a few miles from the place where the first chapel had been."

In the course of a few years, the river lands of the First Acadian coast were completely allotted and assigned to the first-comers. Happy once more were the settlers who received titles to these fertile lands. "On the fall of Canada," says Judge Martin,[8] "A number of the colonists, unwilling to live under their conquerors, sought the warm clime over which the spotless banner still waived; most of them settled in the neighborhood of the Acadians."

Let us note the following letter which was written by the sad and dejected exiles in Georgia to the Duke de Nivernois in 1763. They stated: "For a period of eight years, during which we have been in this country (Georgia) without receiving the Sacraments due to the absence of priests, we have not discontinued saying our prayers in a particular house, and observing Sundays and Holidays as commanded

---

[6] Lauvriere, vol. 2, p. 191, says in 1758.
[7] Lauviere, vol. 2, p. 244.
[8] Quebec fell to the English in Sept., 1759.

by the law of our church, Catholic, Apostolic and Roman."[9] Family prayer was a daily practice, and religious hymns were sung in a low tone of voice in what the exiles considered hostile territory.

By an act of the Louisiana Territorial Legislature, dated April 10, 1805, it was ordained that the county of Acadia "shall comprehend the parishes of St. James and Ascension, commonly called the First and Second Acadian coasts."[10]

Chambers is of the opinion that the first exiles arrived in February, 1765, a band of twenty having reached New Orleans in that month. He states that two hundred thirty from Santo Domingo arrived February 8, 1765, and that they were in a destitute condition. Le Page du Pratz, an early writer, notes that in ascending the Mississippi river in 1767 he passed "two Acadian colonies."[11]

Thomas Ashe, writing in 1806, describes the First and Second Acadian settlements, as follows: "The parish of Cabahanose, or the first Acadian settlement, of eight leagues (24 miles) extent, and further up, a second Acadian settlement, or parish of the Fourche, extending about 6 leagues." Dr. W. A. Read, in his "Louisiana French," p. 153, declares that the name "Cabahanose" was formerly applied to Saint James Parish. In masterly fashion, Dr. Read discusses the origin and meaning of the word "Cabahanosse." It appears that Michel Cantrelle, commandant at Cabahanose for about twenty-eight years, selected this Indian name for his plantation. Dr. Read thinks the word means "mallard roost" or "the wild ducks sleep here." The plantation of Mr. Cantrelle is now known as the "M. B. C." plantation, and is opposite Convent, La.

Louis Judice, who afterwards became commandant of the Second Acadian settlement, as early as October, 1766, used the title "commandant of the Acadians" and performed the duties of his office at Kabahonosse. He continued in this office as such at Kabanhanosse until January, 1772, at which time he began using the title "Commandant and Judge at Lafourche des Chetimaches," to which place he had removed his office. The Second Acadian settlement having been established, and the exiles from Acadia having settled on both banks of the Mississippi in what is now Ascension parish, it became necessary that a commandant and a resident priest take up their posts of duty therein. Commandant Judice continued to serve his fellow-citizens as commandant from January, 1772 to 1797, a period of over twenty-five years. In 1775 he was granted that tract of land immediately above the entrance of Bayou Lafourche, fronting on the Mississippi, and now known as Port Barrow. It is presumed that this was his home

---

9 Lauvriere, vol. 2, p. 108.
10 By an act of the Legislature of Orleans Territory, approved May 31, 1807, this territory was subdivided into 19 parishes. St. James and Ascension formed the sixth and seventh. See the following Acts: Apr. 8, 1824; Feb. 3, 1841; 83 of 1841; 168 of 1842; 130 of 1847; 95 of 1850.
11 Chambers. History of Louisiana, vol. 1, p. 262, 269.

and that he maintained his office therein. Judge Martin, p. 212, says that his duty was to attend to the police of the parish and to preserve peace, to examine all pass-ports and to permit no one to settle here without a license from the governor. He had jurisdiction in small civil cases, acted as notary public, made inventories and conducted sales of deceased persons' estates. He was, therefore, police jury, judge, sheriff and notary.

His death occurred on June 19, 1806, and his mortal remains were interred in the Catholic cemetery in Donaldson town, after church services by Father Boutin. His widow, Marie Jeanne Cantrelle, and two sons survived him.

A view of Houmas Central Factory, at Burnside, Louisiana, once one of the largest sugar factories in South Louisiana. It was demolished a number of years ago and nothing remains of it at this time.

THE SECOND ACADIAN SETTLEMENT—ASCENSION PARISH, LOUISIANA

St. Vincent's Institute, Donaldsonville, La., the oldest educational institution in the Second Acadian Settlement.

FROM far away Acadia, with its beautiful meadows and flocks without number, the exiles kept streaming into southern Louisiana searching for homes in a land which had now become Spanish. Happy were they in the knowledge that their sovereign, Louis XV, and Charles III were closely related, (See La. Hist. Qy. V. 19, No. 1, p. 204) and that they were pledged to aid and assist each other. Into the heart of the Second Acadian settlement they came from Grand Pre, now Wolfville, Port Royal, now Annapolis Royal, Peckouthiac, Piziquid, now the county of Hants, La Pointe de Beausejour, now Fort Cumberland, near Amherst, St. John river, Minca, La Riviere aux Canards, now Kings county, Louisbourg, Quebec, Beaubassin, Miramichi, Maryland, New England, Montreal and St. Malo, France. Weary and worn, they hoped and prayed to find the home of peace and happiness for which they had so long prayed. One hundred seventy-five years have passed into eternity since that gallant band of pioneers first put foot on the soil of the Second Acadian coast.

Longfellow relates the story thus:
"Many a weary year has passed since the burning of Grand Pre,
When on the falling tide the freighted vessels departed,
Bearing a nation, with all its goods, into exile,
Exile without an end, and without an example in story.
. . . Men and women and children, who, guided by hope or by hearsay,
Sought for their kith and their kin among the few-acred farmers
On the Acadian coast . . . ."

An examination of the records of Ascension church and Ascension parish reveal that a considerable number of the exiles had settled in the Second Acadian settlement by the year 1770, and that additional groups came from time to time until about 1790. In their exile, they were indeed "Friendless, homeless, hopeless, they wandered from city to city." Two hundred sixty-seven settlers were found in the District of Lafourche when Governor Alexander O'Reilly took possession of the territory in 1769. Iberville district, including the settlement of Galvez town, contained 375 inhabitants.[12] In view of their great love for France, one can imagine the extent of their grief and disappointment when they learned in 1764 that Louisiana had been ceded by Louis XV to Charles III of Spain. They fervently hoped that it would be only a temporary arrangement, and persisted in the dream that the tri-color of France would some day again wave over Louisiana. In December, 1769, Governor O'Reilly visited the First and Second Acadian settlements and conferred with the leading planters. It is said that they greeted him with "dumb submission."[13] Upon his return to New Orleans, in February, 1770, the governor promulgated regulations under which the home-seekers might acquire titles to the lands on which they had settled. Each settler might obtain a tract of from six to eight arpents front on the Mississippi by a depth of forty arpents, on condition that the grantee would construct a levee, a 40-ft. highway, bridges, and would clear and enclose the entire front to a depth of at least 2 arpents within 3 years from the date of his grant.[14] A settler was prohibited from alienating his holdings until these improvements were made and completed. Boundaries were to be fixed by the commandant in the presence of two adjoining settlers.

Small groups of Acadians continued to wend their way to Louisiana as the years passed. Some of them in France, writing the French King in 1784, petitioned him to grant them leave to join their friends

12 Martin, His. of La., p. 206.
13 Idem, p. 212.
14 Idem, p. 213.

43

and relatives in Louisiana, representing that more than 28 years had elapsed since their expulsion from Acadia, and that they were still in the depths of poverty.[15]

As the year 1785 arrived, we find that the population of New Orleans—today, in truth and in fact America's most interesting city—had grown to 4,980. The First Acadian settlement (St. James parish) was the place of abode of 1332 exiles, while the Second Acadian settlement, or District of Lafourche, contained 646 inhabitants, and Galvez town, on the Amite, numbered 242 inhabitants. The slaves, it appears, outnumbered the free persons.[16] At this date—1785—the curates of Ascension and St. James Catholic churches each received from the government $240. per annum. The curate and sacristan at Galvezton received a larger stipened—$540, plus $50. for expenses.

No figures are available on the population of the ecclesiastical parish of Ascension as of August 15, 1772, the date of the establishment of Ascension Catholic Church with a resident priest, but taking into consideration that at that date 15 years had elapsed since the expulsion of the exiles from Acadia, and considering that in 1785 the settlement contained only 646 inhabitants, it is reasonable to assume that on August 15, 1772 the Second Acadian settlement had a population of approximately 350 persons. The writer is of the opinion that they were nearly all Acadian exiles and their families.

A further increase in population is found in 1785, at which time the census disclosed the following figures: New Orleans, 5338;[17] First Acadian settlement, 1559; Second Acadian settlement, 1164; Galveztown, 268. Judge Francois X. Martin attributes this increase of about 33% to the arrival in Louisiana of about 3500 Acadian exiles.

Mention of the land grants were made to the exiles is discussed in another portion of this book.

---

[15] Lauvriere, vol. 2, p. 199.
[16] Martin, p. 240.

44

Antebellum home of Captain Narcisse Landry,
of Ascension Parish

John Alcide Marchand, Sr., father of the writer, at age 10 years, a
descendant of the Acadian exiles, in a homemade suit of clothing.
Photo taken in 1870.

In Exile A People Build A House of Worship

A DISTINGUISHED Frenchman is authority for the statement that as the Acadians embarked on the British ships—to leave forever their homes, churches and beloved dead—they recited the age-old prayers of the Church, and chanted the hymns heard each Sunday at Mass. It mattered not whether they were dispersed to the north or south, east or west, a firm resolution lurked in each heart to remain faithful to the church of their fathers. History records that they have kept inviolate this resolution. Notwithstanding the fact that their exile, in many cases, extended over a period of years, it is said that they faithfully persisted in the practice of their religion. The indelible picture of the burning of Grand Pre, the church of St. Charles, and other scenes of horror, was not easily forgotten through the years.

First Roman Catholic Church of the Parish of Ascension, 1772

A reconstructed picture of the first church built by the exiles about 1770-72.

The Church of 1770. When the first contingent of Acadians reached southern Louisiana and the Second Acadian settlement (Ascension Parish, Louisiana) they, of course, found no church of any kind at Lafourche des Chetimaches—now Donaldsonville, La. It was not long, however, before these faithful children of the church assembled together with the purpose of devising ways and means of erecting

46

a small house of worship—a chapel. Shortly we see them weilding the axe and the cross-cut saw on the huge trees then standing on the present site of Ascension Catholic church in this city. We see them splitting the great logs into boards, pickets and posts, to be used as building material; short cypress blocks are placed in position, sills, which were made by hand, form the foundation, and the frame, floors, walls, roof are all made from giant trees which, prior to 1770, graced the banks of the Father of Waters. In due time the steeple is built, and the Christian emblem surmounts it. We need not strain our powers of imagination to see the expression of thanks on the faces of the exiles when they expressed their gratitude to the Almighty on first occupying their newly built chapel about the year 1770—six years before the signing of the Declaration of Independence.

The First Acadian settlement (St. James parish, La.), having been settled before the Second Acadian settlement (Ascension Parish), it appears that a Catholic church must have existed at Kabahanosse, in the former settlement, prior to 1770. It is the opinion of the writer, however, that the chapel built in the Second Acadian settlement about 1770 was served by Father Ange de Reuillagodos, as a missionary priest, prior to his taking up his residence here in August, 1772. The following supports this opinion: On December 25, 1771, Commandant Louis Judice conducted a public sale of the estate of Joseph Lincour at the front door of the "parochial church of Assumption" after prayers, which church was situated at Lafourche des Chetimaches; again, when Father Reuillogodos died—Dec. 16, 1784—the entry of a record of his death states that he was pastor of the Ascension Catholic church for 14 years. This would indicate that he served the church as a missionary priest for about two years before he established his residence here—Aug. 15, 1772.

Who selected the site for the church? Who granted the lands? Who determined the extent of the church site? Of this, nothing is known—all, all is forgotten in the annals of the past. Perhaps the questions find sufficient answer in the entry made by Father Reuillogodos when he established his residence here and wrote in his registry:

"On the 15th of August, 1772, I, Father Angelus de Reuillogodos, a member of the order of Capuchins, by order of the Very Reverend Augustine of Toledo, provincial of this Province, and also *by order of His Majesty, King Charles, III,* have taken charge of this parish as first pastor. This parish is dedicated to the Ascension of Our Lord. I have this day witnessed its founding."

The archives of the recorder's office of the parish of Ascension, Louisiana, contain acts passed before Louis Judice, first Spanish commandant of this region, dated as early as May 26, 1769, wherein this officer styles himself "Commandant of the Acadians." These acts were passed by him at Kabahanosse. On April 28, 1770 he refers to himself as "Captain of Militia and Judge of Lafourche des Chetimaches," but he continues to exercise the prerogatives of his office at Kabahanosse (St. James Parish). This convinces the writer that prior to April 28, 1770 some of the Acadians had established themselves at Lafourche des Chetimaches, and that there was no commandant at the latter named place.

When the commissioners, who were appointed by the American government to examine into all private land claims, in 1812, considered the title of the church to the tract in its possession, they commented upon the fact that no written title existed, but that from time immemorial the land had been used for church purposes. They, therefore, recommended that title to the land be confirmed.

No picture of the original church or chapel built by the Acadian exiles in 1770-72 is in existence. Posterity will, therefore, never behold a true and exact likeness of the original structure built by the poor, but God-fearing, Acadian exiles on the present site of the beautiful edifice which now stands at Lafourche des Chetimaches in the Second Acadian settlement. Under these circumstances, and solely for the purpose of giving the writer's general ideas of the appearance of the original church, he has caused an artist to reconstruct a photograph, which is reproduced herein.

The Church of 1781. When the church was first established in the Second Acadian settlement at Lafourche des Chetimaches, settlers were scarce. As an inducement to others to "go west" and join the pioneers, the Spanish government adopted a liberal attitude as to the extent of the grants which it proposed to give to prospective settlers. A church, duly established, exerted considerable influence in bringing the homeseekers to any new settlement. Thus, lands were granted quite freely to the churches. In 1772, when Father Reuillagodos established his ecclesiastical parish of Ascension, the lands of the Church of the parish of Ascension extended from a point 128 ft. east of Railroad avenue to a point about 100 ft. west of what is now Church street, fronting on the river and extending 40 arpents to the rear, as shown on the annexed plat.

The reader will observe that the church lands embraced about two-thirds of the present city of Donaldsonville. Thus, it is noted that on October 5, 1780, Commandant Louis Judice, at the request of Father Reuillagodos, the church wardens and parishioners, offered for sale at public auction at the church door, the upper portion of the church lands, fronting three arpents on the river, by a depth of 40 arpents. It is recited in the act that the land was in excess of church requirements, and that the charges for maintaining roads, levees and bridges were burdensome and excessive to the congregation. The tract was uncultivated and had no fences or buildings thereon. The good Father valued the tract of 120 arpents at $50.; Mathurin Landry appraised it at $100, while Etienne Landry fixed a value of $105. For three successive Sundays the auctioneer wielded all his vocal powers in a sincere effort to get a satisfactory price. On the third Sunday it was sold to Etienne Landry, dit Le Jeune, for $242. The heart of the city of Donaldsonville, La. brought only two dollars per arpent. Did Etienne Landry consider himself fortunate in making this purchase? Did he dream dreams and see visions of the city of Donaldsonville to be built thereon? Evidently not, for on November 12, 1780—just a few weeks following his purchase—he sold the land to Etienne Le Blanc. (Orig. Acts "C," fo. 383).

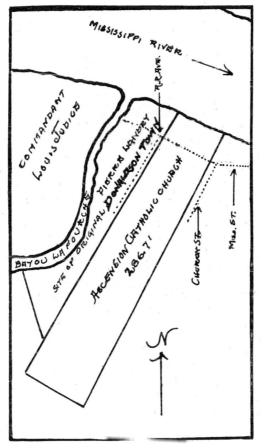

Plat showing lands of Ascension Catholic church, as of 1772.

On September 23rd, 1781, Father Reuillagodos submitted to a meeting of the parishioners a plan for the repair, enlargement and renovation of the original chapel built by the Acadian exiles. Fortunately, a copy of the proces verbal of the deliberations of the assembly held on Sunday, October 14th, 1781, is still in existence. This document reproduced verbatim is as follows:

49

"In the year 1781, Sunday, the 14th day of the month of October, By virtue of the deliberations of all the inhabitants of La Fourche des Chetimaches, assembled at the request of Reverend Father Ange de Reuillagodos, our curate and pastor, in the presbytery of the parish of the Ascension, on the 23rd day of September last, who, having heard the aforesaid Reverend Father make the observation that the church was too small, that each of the parishioners was too cramped during the Holy Sacrifice, that the Sanctuary was also too small, that the curate was obliged to dress before the altar, which was improper in the House of the Lord, and that there was no place to locate a pulpit, in consequence of which he proposed to have the church enlarged by making it thirty feet longer, which said additional thirty feet were necessary in order: Firstly, to enlarge the sanctuary by six feet; secondly, to provide a sacristy of eight feet on the entire width of the proposed added length, and the remaining sixteen feet to go towards enlarging the body of the church.

"The inhabitants, after deliberating among themselves, on the gallery, and having arrived at no decision, we commanded and proposed to the aforesaid, that all those who were in favor of enlarging the church, as was desired by the Reverend Father Ange, to pass into the hall of the presbytery, which they all did at the moment, with the exception of only one, and with one unanimous voice, gave full power to do all the work necessary to lengthen the church and to make all repairs that were to be made, either to the steeple, to the door and windows and the actual church, also to build a pulpit.

"In consequence of the deliberations and general consent of all of the inhabitants, and of the full power to do the work aforementioned, and of the promise of the said inhabitants to furnish so much each to attain and complete the work and the lengthening and other repairs to be made to the ancient church.

"We, Louis Judice, Lieutenant in the army of His Majesty, and commandant and judge of said district of La Fourche des Chetimaches, parish of Ascension, Province of Louisiana, repaired to the front of the principal door of the parochial church of the Ascension of the said "La Fourche," at the time that the high parish mass for the day was being sung and celebrated at the said church; the parishioners and other persons coming out in large numbers in the accustomed manner, we caused to be published and proclaimed in a loud and intelligible voice, that we would presently, in the presence of Reverend Father Ange de Reuillagodos, curate of said parish, proceed for the first time and the first crying out of the adjudication at auction, to the lowest bidder of an addition of thirty feet in length, to be added to the end of the church of the Ascension, on the wood side thereof the entire width of said church, which must be thirty feet in width; which said added length shall be divided as follows: Six feet to enlarge the sanctuary, eight feet to make a sacristy and sixteen feet to enlarge the body of the old church.

"The sacristy shall be separated from the body of the church by a partition of wood and wainscoted in cabinet work.

"There shall be two entrance doors to the church in the sacristy; likewise a third door of exit and two windows in the gable end. On the twenty-two feet which shall comprise the sanctuary and the added length of the church, there shall be three windows on each side with slanting abutments, also make their frames. The contractor or adjudicatee shall make frames for the six windows of the old body of the church. He will reconstruct the large door in order that it shall be arched so that it shall have the appearance of a church door and not that of a prison. The contractor will reconstruct, that is, remodel the steeple and will also build a pulpit, according to the plans that will be given him by the Reverend Father Ange, curate.

"The said contractor and adjudicatee shall be obliged to furnish generally all the lumber for the carpenter work, roof, woodwork, and will likewise do all the carpenter work, woodwork and roofing. He will also build another step to the big altar, the whole of which shall be subject to inspection.

"The contractor shall be required and obliged to furnish generally any and all of the hardware necessary, being the very choice possible of each kind, the paints, which shall be chosen, set the hooks for the windows and doors, and put a good lock on each of the said doors, the whole subject to inspection with all possible exactness.

"The payments shall be made as follows: One quarter at the commencement of the work; the second quarter when the frame shall have been erected and surrounded with bevel-edged planks and the roof put on; the third quarter when the inside of the church shall have been ceiled and all cabinet work done and completed, and the last and final payment as soon as all of the work is finished, inspected and received by experts who shall be named for that purpose.

"Conformably to the publication which we have caused to be made at the capital, and the notice which we have caused to be published at the St. Bernard of Manchack Church, and to the one which we have read, published and posted at the door of this church, and which was read in a loud voice.

"Which said enterprise and furnishings were fixed at the price of Two Thousand Dollars, by Mr. Francois Mollere; and after several crying and having waited more than two hours and no other bidder having presented himself to offer a lower bid on the enterprise, we again announced and published that the present crying was the first and that we would proceed with the same crying in seven days, that is to say, on Sunday, the twenty-first of the present month, we would receive bids on said enterprise, on which day all persons or contractors would be received as bidders and the said enterprise let to the lowest bidder furnishing good and sufficient bond for security of the said enterprise, after which we have closed the present proces verbal, the said day, month and year aforesaid, and have signed.

Signed: LOUIS JUDICE.

In order to recreate a picture of the situation, let us observe the following: The congregation met in the "presbytery"; the pastor noted that the old church was entirely too small; the sanctuary was too small; the curate was obliged to dress at the altar; there was no room for a pulpit. It was proposed to enlarge the building by adding 30 ft. to its length. The congregation could arrive at no decision on the "gallery," and the Father proposed that all of those in favor of the program go inside—and all entered, except one lone objector. The original church had six windows, presumably on each side, and it was about 30 ft. in width; the front door was unsightly. No contract was awarded on Sunday, October 14, 1781, and the matter was deferred to Sunday, October 31, 1781, after High Mass. Here the record is broken, and no further account of the matter is found in the archives of the parish of Ascension. It appears, however, that the contract was awarded to Jacob Cowperthait and Robert Jones, co-partners, their receipt for payment is found, as follows:

"In the year one thousand seven hundred and eighty-three, the 12th day of the month of February:

"Appeared before us, Louis Judice, commandant and judge of Lafource des Chetimaches, Messrs. Robert Jones and Jacob Cowperthwait, contractors of the work of the parochial church of the Ascension, who declared and said and acknowledged and confessed having received from Mr. Pierre Landry, (alias Pitre), church warden of the parochial church of the Ascension at the said "La Fourche," the sum of Twelve Hundred Dollars, in full and complete payment for the work that they did on the said church, in conformity with the adjudication, in faith whereof they gave acquittance and promise to cause to be held acquitted the said Mr. Pierre Landry, as well as all the inhabitants of the said parish.

"In faith whereof they have signed their present declaration with us, at La Fourche des Chetimaches, the day and year aforesaid.

"Signed: JACOB COWPERTHWAIT, ROBERT JONES, *associates*.
"Before me, Commandant: Signed: LOUIS JUDICE."

Less than two years afterwards—December 16, 1784—Father Ange de Reuillagodos, first resident priest and founder of the parish of Ascension, departed this life. (W1-192). An inventory of the small estate of this worthy servant of servants was made by Commandant Louis Judice on January 15, 1785, and his papers and documents were sent to Governor Miro at New Orleans, (A-653; 693), and his remains were interred in the local cemetery by the side of the Acadian exiles he loved and served.

Father Pedro de Zamora assumed control of the affairs of the church of Ascension on Nov. 14, 1784 (W1-192), and he appears to have served until 1789. No record of his death is found.

Father Zamora was succeeded by Father Joseph de Arazena, a native of Andalusia, Spain, who served from 1789 to the date of his death—Aug. 30, 1793. His mortal remains now rest in Ascension Catholic cemetery. Upon the death of Father Arazena, Father Bernardo de Deva, pastor of Assumption church at Valenzuela, assumed control. Between Aug. 30, 1793 and Feb. 12, 1798 we find that Fathers Francois Hotario and Gregory White served. Next came Father John Maguire, who served from 1799 to April 12, 1803; then Father Henry Boutin served to Feb. 25, 1808; then followed Father Charles Lusson, who ministered to his flock from 1808 to the date of his death on Aug. 5, 1812. (W2-2-107). Father Lusson officiated at the funeral of Gaspard Falcon, a Canary Islander, on July 23, 1812, and Father Lusson followed his parishioner on Aug. 4th. Father Bernardo de Deva served the remainder of 1812, to be followed by Fathers D'Epinale, Sibouret and Garcia. Father Thomas Pons assumed the duties of pastor in March, 1816 and served to his death—Aug. 29, 1817—at the age of 47 years. Burial was in the church cemetery. (W2-2-130). Father Huichard succeeded him and served until June, 1818. Then came Father Joseph Tichitoli, who appears to have served as temporary pastor during March and April, 1819, and who returned as pastor in May, 1827. Father Segond Valezano became pastor in July, 1819, and served as such to September, 1821. Our chronology having reached and passed 1819, let us return to the church edifices.

THE CHURCH OF 1819.

Very little is known relative to the appearance of the church built in 1819. On June 14, 1819, the church wardens, Olivier Terriot, Sr., Louis Landry, Paul Landry, Gregoire Dugas and Narcisse Landry, appeared before Philip Carlier D'Outremer, parish judge, and entered into a contract with Francois St. Gees, an architect, wherein the architect obligated himself to build a church for the parish of Ascension, to be located on a site designated by the wardens, in conformity with plans deposited with the clerk of this parish. St. Gees undertook to do all the masonry, carpenter work and painting, and to supply all material necessary. However, he was permitted to cut and use from the church land all necessary timber, and he was also permitted to use church ground with which to make necessary bricks. The building to be of brick throughout. For such a building the wardens obligated themselves to pay $12,500.00, payable one-half in March, 1820, and the remainder in March, 1821. The contract is recorded in C.B. No. 4, fo. 190, of the parish of Ascension, but the plans referred to have never been located. The pastor's name is not mentioned, Commandant Judice—noted for his accuracy and detail—was dead at the time.

Judge Francois Xavier Martin, speaking of Donaldsonville, in 1827, says: "It (Donaldsonville) has an elegant brick church." Thus, it appears that the church of 1819 was built as contemplated in the foregoing contract.

Let us revert for a moment to the church lands. It will be recalled that in October, 1780, the Church of the parish of Ascension, sold at public auction the upper portion of its lands, and that Etienne Landry was the buyer. The tract sold measured three arpents on the Mississippi. By the year 1801, Jean Baptiste Lessard had become the owner of the tract sold to Etienne Landry in 1780. We find that on June 17, 1801, Father John Maguire, cure of the church, sold to William Conway two arpents from the upper portion of the church land, with the full depth. There is some doubt as to whether this two arpent tract is not a portion of the three arpents sold to Etienne Landry in 1780. This land is now in the heart of Donaldsonville, La., and forms that section between Railroad avenue and St. Patrick street. (G-753).

An interesting document—a lease of a farm by the church—is found in C.B. 5, fo. 87, of the Ascension parish records. On March 19, 1821, the church wardens, Silvain LeBlanc, Paul Landry, Louis Landry, Narcisse Landry and Gregoire Dugas, on behalf of the Church of the Parish of Ascension, executed a lease of a "farm" to Antoine Peytavin for a term of twenty-years at $250. per year. It is stipulated in the lease that two arpents front on the river by $7\frac{1}{2}$ in depth, now used as a cemetery, be excluded; and further that Peytavin would keep open a "chemin de charrette" to the rear in order that the cure might be enabled to procure a supply of fire-wood for his use. Failure to pay the rent punctually was cause for annulling the lease. The church authorities evidently decided that the lease was a mistake. The rent became due on March 19, 1822, and Peytavin failed to pay. Suit was filed, and the district court annulled the lease and awarded a penalty of $250. The supreme court reversed this and forced Peytavin to pay rent only. (See, 1 Mart. N.S. 400).

At this point it is well to note the growth of the community, and the changes made in community life since France sold Louisiana to the United States. These epochs are enumerated as follows: William Donaldson, in 1806, purchased the farm of Pierre Landry, to the west or upper side of the original church lands; then Donaldson subdivided the Pierre Landry farm and called his new town "Donaldson"; then a post-office was established "near" Donaldson in 1808, and Thomas Randall was appointed first post-master. The parish no longer has a commandant, but now has a parish judge, and later a police-jury. In September, 1806, we find William Donaldson donating a site for a town hall, and he erects a building at his expense at the south-west corner of the intersection of Chetimaches Street and Nicholls avenue. No longer are auction sales conducted in front of the church, but all sales are made in front of the town hall.

Aside from these changes we note that the planters are fairly prosperous, and large and comfortable homes have replaced the cabins of the exiles in many sections along the First and Second Acadian coasts. The population has increased steadily. Let us scan the figures:

St. James, 1785—1332; 1803—2,200; 1810—3,955.

Ascension, 1785—647; 1803—1,094; 1810—2,219.

The Catholic congregation at Ascension church has steadily increased, and a new church is now in order.

The churches of 1840 and 1875 standing side by side, Donaldsonville, La.

THE CHURCH OF 1840

Many of the old citizens of Ascension parish, Louisiana, and the surrounding country, recall, with a tinge of sadness, the "old church," as they affectionately call the church which was built in 1840. Hundreds living to-day were Christened within its sacred walls, or were joined in the bonds of matrimony before its ancient altar. A lady from Peoria, Ill., journeyed hundreds of miles to Donaldsonville, La. several years ago, in order that she might obtain a photo of the old church or view its ruins. Some of her ancestors had been married there. The picture above shows the church of 1840 to the east or right of the beautiful church of 1875.

In 1840 the Acadian exiles and their descendants took cognizance of the fact that over three-quarters of a century had elapsed since the burning of Grand Pre. Twenty years had elapsed since Architect Francois St. Gees had constructed the church of 1819—the first brick church ever erected within the parish of Ascension, Louisiana. There is some doubt in the mind of the writer as to whether the church of 1840 was a new structure throughout or whether it was a renovation or rebuilding of the church of 1819. If it was an entirely new building, then the old church appears to have been abandoned after only twenty years service. This appears to be a short life for a building constructed of brick. In 1875 the police jury of Ascension parish, Louisiana, declared that the church—meaning the church of 1840—is "in a dilapidated condition, threatening to fall at any day." If the church of 1840 was an entirely new building, it was only 35 years of age at the time the police jury made these remarks. The reader will reach his own conclusion.

The recorder's office of Ascension parish gives no light on the church of 1840. However, from a decision of the supreme Court of Louisiana, (6 Rob. 532) we glean the following: Contractor Volquin was employed by the congregation to build the church; Volquin employed Claudet Dumont to roof the edifice for $1,650, slate being required, but later changed to zinc. The architect certified that the roof job was completed, but the wardens declined to pay as they had already paid Volquin in full. The court sustained their contention. Volquin's contract called for a completed job at $19,000, payable $1,000 monthly beginning Apr. 1, 1840. The roof was completed in December, 1841. The supreme court finally reversed the district court.

It was probably 1843, or thereabout, before the edifice was completed. The turrets were not erected until 1847, for on Jan. 7, 1847, P. G. Dannequin, treasurer, advertised as follows:

"Notice to contractors. Sealed proposals will be received by the undersigned until the 28th inst. for the erection of two turrets on the parish church, which must be constructed according to the plan which will be exhibited when required."

Mr. Dannequin also announces that a portion of the church land, not exceeding 100 arpents, will be sold at public auction on Jan. 30, 1847. The "old church" standing alone is shown below:

Closely associated with the church in the century that has elapsed since the church of 1840 was built, is St. Vincent's Institute, at Donaldsonville, La. A hundred years have ceased to be since Sisters Loretto, Mary Gonzaga, Paschal, Sevina, Theonelle and Adelaide arrived in Donaldsonville, Louisiana. Upon their arrival they took possession of a house of four small rooms, which they used as a parlor, domitory, schoolroom and community room. January 1, 1843 marked

The Catholic church built by the exiles and their descendants at Donaldsonville, La. in 1840.

their arrival. The town at that time had "a court house, jail, arsenal, market house, a Roman Catholic church, a college, one male and two female academies, a United States Surveyor-General's office, and about one thousand population." The corporation limits extended east and west from Bayou Lafourche to St. Patrick Street.

On Oct. 11, 1847 Edward Duffel, Sr., Jean Bouillier, Narcisse Landry, Edward Gaudin, Pierre Gontran Dannequin, William Hatkinson and Albert Duffel, church wardens of the Roman Catholic church of Ascension, declared that by and under the authority of an act of Legislature, approved Mar. 14, 1844, they donated to the Sisters of Charity of the order of St. Vincent de Paul, represented by Sisters Mary Loretta, Mary Angelina, and Mary Austin, a portion of the plantation owned by the church, bounded above by the town of Donaldsonville and below by the plantation of Valery Landry, containing seven arpents, together with a certain lot on St. Patrick street, said property to be used as a site for a hospital, a school and an asylum for orphan girls. (See C.B. 21, fo. 70).

On September 5, 1897 said donation was revoked in part, and it was noted that Sisters Mary Loretta, Mary Angelina and Mary Austin are all now deceased, and that they were succeeded by Sisters Mary

Clothilde, Mary Angelica, Miriam and Juliana. (See C.B. 79, fo. 363; Act 94 of 1874; Act 177 of 1848).

On March 16, 1848, the Legislature appropriated $5,000 to the Sisters, and "The Vigilant," of June 3, 1848, contains a news-item to the effect that Archbishop A. Blanc attended the ceremonies in connection with the laying of the cornerstone of the hospital. The hospital and asylum continued to operate for "a number of years," but was no longer so used in 1897.

Recently, St. Vincent's celebrated its centennial. A pageant depicting the principal events of its long life was presented, and a solemn high Mass was celebrated in Ascension church with Archbishop Rummel, Bishops Gerow, of Natchez, and Jeanmard, of Lafayette, and a large number of visiting priests in attendance.

THE CHURCH OF 1875

A hundred years have now elapsed since the Acadian exiles first gazed upon the wild and undeveloped lands of the First and Second Acadian settlements. Ascension parish now has a population of 11,577, and all are free—there are no slaves. Donaldsonville boasts a population of 1,600. Father Francis Xavier Ceuppens, a native of Belgium, is now pastor of Ascension Catholic church. The church which was built in 1840 is getting old, and is too small for the growing congregation. Some ten years have elapsed since the Civil War ended, and the planters are getting back "on their feet." Father Ceuppens, probably dreaming of the beautiful churches in distant Belgium, Germany and Italy, decided the time was at hand to build such an edifice in the Second Acadian settlement at Lafourche des Chetimaches. In 1875 he aroused the congregation to the necessity of such a church, and made a start. In July, 1878, he stated to the town council of Donaldsonville that he was building a "new church which will be an ornament to the town." A volume could be written on the church of 1875; the expulsion of Father Ceuppens from the town by a dissatisfied minority of his congregation; the closing of the church of 1840 by an order of Court, and finally, of the successful completion by Father Dubernard and dedication of the great structure, when hundreds journeyed long distance to witness the solemn event. It was on Tuesday, April 14, 1896—more than twenty years after the foundations were laid—that Archbishop Janssens dedicated it as a House of Worship. When dedicated, the structure was not entirely completed. Father Dubernard saw the completion of the edifice in 1900. Father Ceuppens lived to see the dedication, but not the completion of the church, having departed this life at Hotel Dieu, New Orleans, on July 20, 1897. A view of the edifice from the intersection of Iberville and St. Vincent streets, is shown on the next page.

58

Ascension Catholic Church, Donaldsonville, La. View from Iberville and
St. Vincent Streets.

THE CHURCH AT LA RIVIERE NEUVE.

From time to time during the first years of the 19th century, probably between 1830 and 1855, some of the Acadians and their descendants—the Landry's, Le Blancs, Gautreaus, Melancons, Babins, Heberts, Marchands and Boudreaux—penetrated into the wild and undeveloped section forming the northern and eastern portion of the Second Acadian settlement, then known as La Riviere Neuve or New River. Today we find there the progressive town of Gonzales and a dozen hamlets and settlements, modern schools, roads and other conveniences. Whence came the name "New River"? The name "Nouvele Riviere" appears on a map of the county of Acadia, dated 1805, reproduced herein. Thus, while we may call the little winding stream "new," it appears that it is at least 135 years of age. Further, in 1840 there was a post-office known as New River which was situated at what is now Geismar, La.

All of the original Acadian exiles who settled in the Second Acadian settlement (now Ascension parish) during the years 1768 to 1785, settled on the banks of the great old Mississippi river. Ancient maps, land-transactions and other contracts show that fact beyond a doubt. The country now known as "New River" was probably unknown to the settlers for a number of years. Thereupon, came hunters who penetrated further and further north into the swamps and cane-brakes to see and inspect the terrain. Suddenly a small stream comes into view, and it is not the Amite, Iberville or Riviere des Acadians. To the settlers it was a "new" river, and to this date the name has stuck to the fair little stream—the old swimming hole of the writer, Lester E. Wright, Sr., Allen Landry, Ulysse Braud, F. Harold Marchand, John . Marchand, Jr., Denery Picard, Rudolph, Hector and Estress Braud, Warren, Andrew and Leslie Le Blanc. Nor should we forget the marvelous "peerches" which these juvenile fisherman brought forth from the depths—at least 3 ft.—of old New River.

By 1850, we find scattered settlements on the banks of New River, and the majority are of the Catholic faith. Thus, in 1864, Father Lessaicherre established a small chapel in the upper part of New River settlement at a point later known as Cornerview. The church was named Sacred Heart Catholic church. This was the first Catholic church, with a resident priest, in the New River section, and the second oldest Catholic church in Ascension parish. Some twenty years ago it was discontinued as a parish church with a resident priest, as churches had been established at Prairieville, Gonzales and St. Amant. The body of the old church still stands.

THE CEMETERY OF THE EXILES.

The exact location of the cemetery of the church of the Ascension used by the Acadian exiles and their descendants, is a matter of interest, and should be noted here. It is the writer's opinion that the church has been, continuously from 1772 to the present time, located at or near the site of the present church. The burial ground of the exiles was adjacent to the original church. It has already been noted that on March 19, 1821, the church wardens leased a "farm"—part of the church property—to Antoine Peytavin. A tract measuring two by seven and one-half arpents, used as a cemetery, is expressly excluded from the lease. This refers to the burial ground used by the exiles, and it was probably at, or very near, the site of the present church. Let us bear in mind the following: (1) When the church of 1875 was begun numerous bodies were removed from the church site, and (2) The oldest person living in Donaldsonville does not recall a time when the church used any cemetery other than that presently used, and situated between St. Vincent, Opelousas and Church streets. Placide Ramirez, an old citizen who departed this life about eight years ago, stated to the writer that he actually worked on the foundations of the church of 1875, and that Father Ceuppens required that the entire site of the church be excavated to a depth of 6 feet and that all human remains be removed to the cemetery presently used. The writer has been told that when the sewer lines were laid on St. Vincent street, near Mississippi street, about 1932, human bones were found on several occasions. To summarize the matter, we may say that in 1875 the present Catholic cemetery was an old burial ground, but that a still older one existed on the site of the church of 1875; and that the older cemetery was probably the burial ground of the Acadian exiles. Below is a photo of the tomb of Thomas Randall, which is situated in the cemetery presently used. Mr. Randall was the first postmaster at Donaldson Town, and died in 1808. A photograph of the Bringier tomb—age about 60 years—is also reproduced herein below.

Tomb of Thomas Randall, first postmaster at Donaldson Town. His death occurred on July 12, 1808, about thirty days after he was appointed.

Hotel Donaldson, erected 108
years after founding of town.

The Bringier tomb, wherein is interred the remains of Duncan F. Kenner, distinguished statesman.

First Officials of The Second Acadian Settlement

Commandant Louis Judice.—Spanish Governor, Alexander O'Reilly took possession of Louisiana on August 18, 1769. He had suppressed the revolting settlers, and now undertook the laborious work of transforming them into veritable Spaniards. All settlers had to present themselves to their respective commandants to take the oath of allegiance. At that date the territory now comprising Ascension parish had no resident commandant. However, we find that Louis Judice, the first public official ever to reside within the limits of Ascension parish, as early as October 14, 1766 was officiating as commandant of the Acadians at Kabahanoce, now St. James parish. (Orig. Acts, "Q," fo. 723). He used the title "commandant of the Acadians" from his office at Kabahanoce or Cabahanose during the years 1767, 1768 and 1769. On November 25, 1769, Governor O'Reilly created several new commandants, and it is presumed that the territorial jurisdiction of Louis Judice was extended and enlarged at that time. Thus, on April 28, 1770, we find him using the title "Captain of militia and Judge of Lafourche des Chetimaches," though he continued to maintain his office at Cabahanoce. (Orig. Acts "Q," fo. 659). The settlers in the Second Acadian settlement were now becoming more numerous and the grand old man has decided to remove his office to Lafourche des Chetimaches—now Donaldsonville, La. Judice established himself here about thirty-five years before William Donaldson established his Donaldson Town. Hence, on January 9, 1772, he began using the title "Commandant and Judge of Lafourche des Chetimaches," and he is now maintaining his office at this location. The records indicate that he pitched his "tent"—built a small cabin—on the tract of land now forming the village of Port Barrow, opposite the city of Donaldsonville. This tract was granted to him by Governor Unzaga on November 5, 1775. It had a frontage on the Mississippi river of 11 arpents. His son, Michel Judice, settled on the tract just above his father. The first public official of the parish of Ascension built on his wooded tract a small cabin measuring 27′ x 16′. (Orig. Acts "F," fo. 887). On Sept. 30, 1800 he sold this tract to Jacob Bobbs. ("F," fo. 887). His service as commandant of Ascension parish extended from 1770 to 1798—over a quarter of a century. His official acts attest his liberal education. Though he was a Spanish commandant during all of this period, he used the French language exclusively in all of his acts of sale, mortgages, inventories, etc. His first wife

63

was Marie Jeanne Cantrelle of Cabahanose, probably a daughter or sister of Michel Cantrelle, once commandant at St. James parish and first county judge of Acadia county. His first wife departed this life on September 25, 1794, and on June 19, 1795 he was married to Marie Henrietta Rossicot, the widow of Pierre Le Compte.

COMMANDANT EVAN JONES.—The second Spanish commandant to serve at Lafourche des Chetimaches was Don Evan Jones. In the old records he is described as being a "negociant"—a merchant or broker—of New Orleans. He was appointed commandant of this region prior to October 2, 1797, and continued to hold the office as late as September, 1798. An ancestor of the McCall family of Evan Hall plantation, McCall, La., he was a prominent citizen and planter of the old days, but to-day, a century and a half afterwards, it is not believed that a single member of his distinguished family resides within the parish of Ascension.

Desire Le Blanc, (an Acadian exile and probably an ancestor of Chief of Police, Louis L. Le Blanc, and of Leo L. Le Blanc, Sr.), whose descendants to-day are found in every nook and corner of Ascension parish, settled on a tract of woodland at what is now the front portion of Evan Hall plantation. At the death of Desire Le Blanc he was survived by his widow, Marie Landry, and a large number of children. When his landed estate was sold it was purchased by his son, Simon Le Blanc, and at the death of the latter Evan Jones acquired the property—his acquisition being dated Sept. 16, 1778. Jones later acquired other adjoining tracts and laid the foundation of the much-admired Evan Hall plantation.

It is not known how long Evan Jones resided in Ascension parish, or whether he resided here at all. At the time of the marriage of his daughter, Lise Jones, to Henry McCall, "The Courier" of New Orleans, of May 28, 1807, announced: "Married, on Saturday evening the 24th inst. by the Reverend Father Antoine, Mr. Henry McCall to Miss Lise Jones, daughter of Evan Jones, Esq., all of this city."

Another daughter, Marie Jones, married Bernard Marigny, a prominent citizen of New Orleans, and left at her decease two sons, Prosper and Gustave Marigny. Marie Verret, the widow of Evan Jones, died prior to August 30, 1821. (C.B. 8, fo. 157). In "The Gazette," of New Orleans, of Feb. 14, 1812, Evan Jones advertised as follows: "Eighty hogshead of country sugar, of the first quality, to be sold by Evan Jones."

He died about 1812, and his succession was opened in New Orleans. (Orig. Acts "P," fo. 57). At the sale of his estate on Nov. 28, 1818, his widow, Marie Verret, purchased his plantation, now "Evan Hall." On Jan. 13, 1819, she sold an undivided one-half thereof to her son-in-law, Henry McCall. Mr. McCall died on May 22, 1859, leaving three sons, Richard, Henry, Jr., and Evan Jones McCall.

In "The Donaldsonville Chief" of Aug. 19, 1882 the following tribute is paid Henry McCall:

"We now come to Evan Hall, . . . Henry McCall, a gentleman of the old school, owned the "Hall" as far back as can be remembered, for scarcely one has ever heard of Evan Jones, his father-in-law . . . .

"The commodious brick warehouse, large saw-mill, lordly mansion, with its terraced and well-kept front yard, splendid two-story store, magnificent sugarhouse and unsurpassed machinery, other buildings, trim fences, railroad, etc., etc., all attest that the Hall is unexcelled by any other sugar estate of the country in attractiveness of its appearance and the value and usefulness of its improvements." (See "Flight of a Century, p. 211).

COMMANDANT RAFAEL CROQUER.—Evan Jones was succeeded as commandant of Lafourche des Chetimaches by Dr. Rafael Croquer, a Spanish scholar. He began serving on October 5, 1798. All of his official acts are written in Spanish. It appears that he held this office during the years 1799, 1800, 1801, 1802, 1803 and the early part of 1804. When Dr. John Watkins, personal representative of Governor Claiborne, visited this section in 1804 to contact all commandants, he called upon Mr. Croquer. In his report to the Governor, he states: "This district was formerly governed by Mr. Croquer, an officer attached to the Spanish service, who in consequence of this circumstance was obliged though very reluctantly to decline accepting a re-appointment." Details concerning his family, place of birth, and date and place of marriage and death are unknown.

COMMANDANT JOSEPH LANDRY.—Following the purchase of the Louisiana territory by the United States of America, in December, 1803, it was necessary that the American governor, W. C. C. Claiborne, appoint capable and trustworthy commandants in the out-lying districts, as hereinbefore stated. Don Rafael Croquer was in the military service of Spain and could not accept re-appointment. Dr. Watkins, in his report to the governor, states:

"In choosing his successor . . . . I kept constantly in view the instructions of Your Excellency. After having made myself personally acquainted with many of the principal characters of the parish, and consulted a great number of the inhabitants, I commissioned, in the place of Mr. Croquer, Mr. Joseph L'Andry, a wealthy farmer and the person who had always acted as commandant per interim during the absence of Mr. Croquer.

"This gentleman altho born in Acadia, has resided many years in Louisiana, speaks the English and French languages, professes strong attachment to the government of the United States, and possesses the unlimited confidence and affection of all the inhabitants of the district in which he lives."

On the recommendations of his people and of Dr. Watkins,

Joseph Landry was appointed by Governor Claiborne in the early part of 1804 as the first American commandant at Lafourche des Cheti-maches. He held this post for a little over one year, for on May 20, 1805, Governor Claiborne wrote him:

"A law of the Territory directs that first and second Acadian coasts shall compose a county, and that a judge for the same shall be appointed, to whom certain duties now vested in you as commandant, shall be confided.

"In conformity to the law I have appointed Mr. Michel Cantrelle, the most ancient commandant in the territory, and I request that you would deliver to him the papers and records of your parish. I have nominated you a justice of the peace, and left your commission with Mr. Cantrell. . ."

He served as justice of the peace for some time after June 15, 1805, but the old commandant could not forget this rebuff, and it is said that he bitterly resented the demotion. He became a candidate, and was elected to the Territorial Legislature in September, 1805. Prior to June 15, 1806, however, he had resigned from this office. Governor Claiborne ordered an election to choose his successor. In July, 1812, he was elected a member of the state senate from the county of Acadia, while his son-in-law, Stephen A. Hopkins, was elected to the house of representatives. Senator Landry was greatly disappointed at the re-election of Governor Claiborne, and he declined to accept his seat in the senate.

A pen portrait of Joseph Landry, the Acadian exile who became a recognized leader in the "Golden Coast," is found in "The Donaldsonville Chief" of Aug. 19, 1882. This picture and tribute is as follows:

"We have now reached the second district, and the first place in it is 'Home,' and well has it been so named, for it was during a long time the nest, as it were, from which whole generations of the Landry family took their flight. (See 20 Ann. 359).

"Among the Acadians who found rest in this country from the cruelties of the English people, was Joseph Landry, dit le Bel, who founded 'Home.' Under the Spanish government (sic) he held the position of El Commandante del distrito, and was a man of worth. He, his wife, his sons, Louis, Achille, Joseph, Narcisse, Valery and Trasimond are dead. He was succeeded on 'Home' by his son, Achille, and this one by his brother, Governor, Colonel Trasimon Landry, as he was indifferently named, who lived to a good old age and who, while in his seventies, marched with the armies of the Confederacy to the end of the war. A more hospitable gentleman never lived; and a more courteous one to everybody, and more gallant to the fair sex, it were difficult to have found. After his death, 'Home' was purchased successively by Dr. Wilkinson, Col. Barrow, Capt. Borland and Gen. Allen Thomas, who are now all living in other portions of the state. The plantation finally fell to the ownership of the millionaire, John

Burnside, who bequeathed it to its present owner. (Oliver Beirne).

" 'Home' is a sacred and holy spot to many persons of this and other parishes. In its substantial mansion house many were brought into this world; many were there given in marriage, and many were carried from it to their last resting place. Besides those already named, others have followed their steps to the distant bourne, viz: Amedee, Gustave, Theodule, Samuel, John Landry—there to join others again, Mrs. Pedesclaux, Mrs. Poursine, Mrs. Dernon Le Blanc, Mrs. Judge Ed. Duffel, Mrs. Tournillon, Mrs. Martin, Mrs. Beamon. Trasimon was owner of seven or eight tracts of land, all under cultivation, and vast sections of forest lands, and now his descendants, like King John of England, are sans terre.

"Sic transit, etc. But after all what boots it that one should own land? His manhood and integrity are his own, which no power can strip him of, and when these remain, all is not gone. The father of Joseph Landry snatched from the rivers and tides those alluvial marshes of exuberant fertility in Nova Scotia, which excited the cupidity of the 'Lords of Trade,' and when Grand Pre, and Beausejour and Baivard were wrestled from the possession of the Acadians, Joseph Landry and neighbors sought the then western wilds, subdued the great Mississippi river, levelled the tangled forests of oaks and cypresses, and caused to bloom beneath the sun the richest lands of the globe. Let the new generation then, by dint of industry, perseverance and frugality, recover their lost inheritances or carve unto themselves new estates, which will surpass in splendor the old possessions."

Joseph Landry was twice married, first to Isabelle Le Blanc, and then to Anna Bujol. He departed this life on Oct. 11, 1814, and his mortal remains were laid to rest in Ascension Catholic cemetery at Donaldsonville. Upon the occasion of his funeral, Father Bernardo de Deva inscribed upon his records the following tribute to Mr. Landry: "A member of the senate and legislature, husband of Anna Bujol, a good husband, a good citizen and possessed of all Christian virtues." His descendants are legion, and are found in various sections of Louisiana.

Spanish Land Grants to Acadian Exiles

THE Spanish government granted to all the early settlers—principally Acadian exiles—tracts of land on both banks of the Mississippi and Amite rivers, as well as on Bayou LaFourche. Very few grants were made by the Spanish Government for lands in the interior, though there are a number of such grants, such as the John Alman grant at Prairieville, Louisiana—to this day known as Alman's prairie. However, in nearly all cases, the early settlers selected lands on the banks of the rivers, streams and bayous. The whereabouts of the original Spanish land grants seem to be unknown to Louisiana historians. None of the originals are on file in the Ascension parish, Louisiana, court-house. They are merely referred to in the various acts hereinbelow cited. The following abbreviations are used: 4 arp., indicates 4 arpents front on the Mississippi river; RBMR, indicates the right or west bank of the Mississippi River; LBMR indicates the left or east bank of the river. LNO means "Leagues above New Orleans." A league, of course, is 3 miles. The following Spanish grants are specifically referred to:

Date		Grantee	Property
1765			
Nov.	3	Gregoire French, LBMR, 20 arp. front, 24 LNO, Houmas.	
1770			
Apr.	2	Jacque La Chance, 23 LNO.	
1774			
Feb.	22	Francois Simoneaux, 11 arp. bet. Evan Jones & Claude Le Blanc.	
1775			
Nov.	5	Simon Landry, 12 arp., bet. Pierre Landry & Bapt'e. Braud.	
Nov.	5	Isaac Le Blanc, LBMR, bet. Chas. Melancon & Jos. Landry.	
Nov.	5	Paul Melancon, LBMR, bet. Chas. Melancon & Jos. Landry.	
Nov.	5	Paul Braud, LBMR, 5 arp. bet. Bte. Braud and Bte. Landry.	
Nov.	5	Jos. Babin, dit Dios, RBMR, bet. Pierre Landry & Chas. Lincour.	
Nov.	5	Chas. Forrest, 6 arpt.	
Nov.	5	Etienne Landry, 6 arp. LBMR, 27 LNO.	
Nov.	5	Jean Baptiste Chauvin, 11 arp.	
Nov.	5	Amand Gautros, 6 arp., bet. Vincent and Pierre Landry.	
Nov.	5	Etienne Bujol, 5 arp.	
Nov.	5	Pierre Bujol, 5 arp.	
Nov.	5	Etienne Landry, dit Lejeune, 5 arp.	

Date		Grantee	Property
Nov.	5	Rene Landry, 5 arp., LBMR, opp. Bayou Lafourche.	
Nov.	5	Jacque Landry, 8 arp.	
Nov.	5	Desire Le Blanc, 8 arp., RBMR, bet. Jos. Bujol & Jerome Le Blanc.	
Nov.	5	Jos. Bujol, 5 arp. RBMR, bet. Jean Bujol & Evan Jones.	
Nov.	5	Firmin Broussard, 4 arp., LBMR, 1 league ab. Church.	
Nov.	5	Chas. Melancon, 7 arp.	
Nov.	5	Louis Judice, 4 arp., Bayou Lafourche, near river.	
Nov.	5	Pierre Landry, dit Pitre, site of Donaldsonville, La.	

1777

July	10	Olivier Landry, 5 arp., LBMR.	
Nov.	20	Firmin Broussard, 6 arp., LBMR.	

1785

Jan.	1	Thos. Lillewhite (Heliote), 12 arp. LBMR, 28 LNO.	
Feb.	7	Paul Landry, 5 arp., LBMR, bet. Widow Landry and Enselme Le Blanc.	

1785—William Conway, at Bayou des Ecores.
1785—Joseph Guedry, 4 arp., LBMR, bet. Firmin Guedry & Hy. Kling.
1785—Basil Landry, 5 arp., RBMR, 23 LNO, Gov. Unzaga.
1785—Enselme Belisle, 5 arp., RBMR, 25 LNO.
1875—Enselme Blanchard, 6 arp., bet. Paul Chaisson to Ignace Babin.
   Charles Forest, Jr., 6 arp., RBMR, 24 LNO.
   Charles Bergeron, 4 arp., LBMR, bet. Pierre Carmouche and Basil Prejean.

1789

Sept.	26	Louis LeComte, 8 arp., RBMR, L'isle aux Marais.	
Sept.	28	Pierre Le Comte, 8 arp., RBMR, L'isle aux Marais.	

1790

Dec.	29	Nil Macdonno, 7 arp., LBMR, 28 LNO.	
		Nicolas Doublin, 6 arp., LBBL, 1½ mi., from Gov. Miro.	
Oct.	8	Silvain Le Blanc, 6 arp., RBMR, 2½ leagues ab. church.	

1796

Dec.	12	Jean Bte. Seizan, arp., LBMR, ab. by Rousin, bel. by Michel Braud.	

1797

Aug.	9	Bonaventure Babin, 11 arps.	

1797—Pierre Landry, dit Pierrot a Jacque, 6 arp. Houmas.
   Claude Duhon, 5 arp., RBMR, 23 LNO.
   Ursule Landry Babin, 4 arp.
   Francois Duhon, 6 arp., LBMR, 24 LNO.
   Marin Prejean, 4 arp., RBMR, 23 LNO.
   Etienne Landry, 6 arp., LBMR, 26 LNO.
   Jean Duhon, 6 arp., RBMR, 23 LNO.
   Jean Bte. Braud, 19 arp., LBMR, 24 LNO.
   Simon Landry, 9 arp., LBMR.

Date   Grantee   Property
    Firmin Dupuis, 4 arp., LBMR, 28 LNO.
    Enselme Blanchard, RBMR, bet. Honore Braud & Jos. A.
    Landry.
    Pierre Landry, 6 arp., RBMR, bet. Jos. Landry & Usebe Landry.
    Pierre Bore, 6 arp., bet. Michel Verret & Bte. Blanchard.
1804
June 15 Edward Gaudin, 1 arp., RBMR, 2 leagues ab. church.

Firemen's Parade, Donaldsonville, about 1905.

THE FIRST FIVE HUNDRED NATIVE BORN CITIZENS OF ASCENSION PARISH, LOUISIANA

Name	Parents	Date of birth
Jerome Raymond Braud	Paul, & Marie Marthe Le Blanc	Aug. 28

1772

Name	Parents	Date of birth
Edward Le Blanc	Simon, & Anne Arceneaux	May 2
Anna Braud	Athanas, & Marie Le Blanc	May 15
Emanuel Rodriguez	Antonio, & Cecile P. Duhon	June 18
Paul Hebert	Pierre, & Marguerite Babin	Aug. 8
Francoise Landry	Aman, & Marguerite Melancon	Aug. 9
Jacque Chevalier	Jean, & Marie Perrin	Aug. 19
Ceaser Terrio	Thomas, & Angele Daigle	Aug. 27
Paul Francois Chauvin	Jean Chauvin, (illegible)	Oct. 4
Louis Dumini Belard	Antoine, & Marie Trahan	Nov. 5
Jean Louis Landry	Pierre, & Marie Landry	Oct. 11
Francois Braud	Firmin, & Marguerite Braud	Nov. 28*
Simon Gautreau	Simon, & Magdeleine Braud	Aug. 22
Martin Louis Broussard	Augustin, & Anne Landry	Nov. 11
Francois Muro	Francois, & (illegible)	Nov. 22*
Marie Joseph Orillion	Joseph, & Marie Rose Braud	Nov. 19
Jean Baptiste Faltement	Laurent, & Marie Marobre	Nov. 28
Felicite Prejean	Aman, & Magdelene Martin	Dec. 11
Anastasie Landry	Mathurin, & Pelagie Landry	Dec. 24
Anastasie Rosalie Landry	Mathieu, & Anna Landry	Dec. 24

1773

Name	Parents	Date of birth
Marie Louise Butie	Michel, & Marie Rose (illegible)	Jan. 3
Anna Poulonne Landry	Jacque, & Francoise Blanchard	Jan. 21
Charles Duhon	Charles, & Marie Landry	Jan. 27
Louis Prejean	(illegible) & Marie Joseph Gaudin,	Jan. 30
Pierre Baptiste Landry	Rene, & Anne Landry	Feb. 6
Jacque Le Blanc	Pierre, & Anne Landry	Mar. 24
Marie Babin	Joseph, & Marie Landry	Mar. 27
Marie Magdelene Landry	Simon, & Marguerite Babin	Mar. 30
Anselm Braud	Paul, & Marie Marthe Le Blanc	Apr. 20
August Victor Constant	Joseph, & Marguerite Bujol	May 6
Marie Sophie Gautreau	Aman, & Marie Landry	June 9
Marie Magdeline Babin	Joseph, & Ositte Le Blanc	June 15
Marie Isabel Melancon	Charles, & Felicite Landry	June 19
—————Landry	Etienne, & Marie Landry	June 21
—————Benoit	Etienne, & Magdelene Braud	June 21
Simon Pierre Granger	Joseph, & Genevieve Babin	July 20
Simon Rafael Babin	Aman, & Anatasie Landry	Aug. 19
Marie Julia Duhon	Francois, & Isabel Landry	Aug. 23
Athanas Dugas	Francois, & Marg'te Babin	Sept. 20
Marie Francoise Dugas	Charles, & Rosa Babin	Oct. 11

Name	Parents	Date of birth
Gregoire Rafael Landry	Joseph, & Anne Granger	Oct. 23
Felicite Foret	Paul, & Marguerite Orillion	Nov. 23
Clemence Anne Foret	Paul, & Marguerite Orillion	Nov. 23
Marie Baptiste Chauvin	Jean Baptiste, & Marguerite Braud	Nov. 29
Simon Pierre Prejean	Charles, & Marguerite Richard	Dec. 24

1774

Name	Parents	Date of birth
Joseph Beloni Babin	Firmin, & Bibiana Braud	Jan. 12
Marie Sophie Le Blanc	Isaac, & Marie Melancon	Jan. 21
Isabel Lincour	Charles, & Marie Joseph Babin	Jan. 28
Marie Elizabeth Landry	Vincent, & Suzanne Gaudin	Feb. 8
Marie Magdeline Le Blanc	Silvin, & Marie Joseph Babin	Mar. 5
Joseph Hebert	Prosper Hebert & Marie Dupuy	Mar. 14
Marie Madgeline Babin	Charles, & Magdelene Babin	Mar. 17
Pierre Castel Braud	Firmin, & Marguerite Braud	Mar. 31
Joseph Halard	Jean B. & Marie C. Puriho	May 8
Francois Babin	Francois, & Marguerite Braud	May 9
Joseph Duhon	Jean Duhon & Anne Le Blanc	Mar. 7
Julienne Therese Landry	Marine Landry-Pelagie Landry	May 18
Petronelle Victorine Babin	Efrem, & Marguerite LeBlanc	May 28
Louis Braud	Joseph, & Marie Joseph Landry	June 17
Uzelle Braud	Joseph, & Marie Jos. Landry	June 17
Pierre Alexis Landry	Simon, & Marguerite Babin	July 18
Paul Eusebe Landry	Pierre, & Marie Landry	Aug. 14
Marie Louise Le Blanc	Pierre, & Anna Landry	Sept. 9
Joseph Nicolas Landry	Maturin, & Anne Landry	Sept. 10
Ann Constance Constant	Joseph, & Marguerite Bujol	Oct. 3
Marie Christine Landry	Augustin, & Ana Marie Foret	Oct. 4
Marie Bujol	Augustin, & Gertrude Landry	Oct. 11
Dominic Prejean	Aman, & Marie Therriot	Oct. 20
Joseph Efrem Babin	Joseph, & Osite Le Blanc	Nov. 1
Victoire Constance Landry	Pierre, & Marguerite Allain	Nov. 2
Marie Magdelene Foret	Anselm, & Marie Magdelene Le Blanc	Nov. 17
Joseph Broussard	Augustin, & Anne Landry	Nov. 18
Ana Adelaide Duhon	Francois, & Isabel Landry	Oct. 25
Chas. Gregoire Dugas	Charles, & Rose Babin	Dec. 20
(Illegible) Simoneaux	Francois, & Marie Corporen	Dec. 28

1775

Name	Parents	Date of birth
Marie Magdelene Braud	Paul, & Narie Marthe LeBlanc	Jan. 8
Guillaume Landry	Joseph, & Anna Granger	Jan. 10
Jacques Babin	Aman, & Anatasie Landry	Jan. 12
Marguerite Andro	Francois, & Genevieve Hebert	Jan. 16
Firmin Paul Landry	Firmin, & Louise Div. Babin	Jan. 16
Marie Euphrene Granger	Joseph, & Genevieve Babin	Feb. 6
Joseph Orillion	Joseph, & Marie Rose Braud	Feb. 6
Marguerite Marine Hebert	Jean Hebert & Marguerite Richard	Feb. 25
Marie Magdelene Richard	Simon, & Marie Rose Landry	Apr. 4
Paul Babin	Joseph, & Osite LeBlanc	May 12
Marie Angele Benoit	Etienne, & Magdelene Braud	June 14
Jean Baptiste Melancon	Charles, & Felicite Landry	June 17
Marie Marine Duhon	Charles, & Marie Joseph Prejean	Aug. 9

Name	Parents	Date of birth
Rosalie Gallien	Joseph, & Marie Bouten	Aug. 12
Theodore Gautreau	Aman, & Marie Landry	Sept. 3
Marguerite Belisle	Enselm, & Marie Joseph Dupuy	Sept. 12
Jean Nicolas Landry	Jean, & Anne Marie Le Blanc	Sept. 15
Joseph Landry	Etienne, & Marie Landry	Sept. 21
Madeleine Prejean	Charles, & Marguerite Richard	Oct. 8
Paul Babin	Joseph, & Marine Le Blanc	Nov. 20
Marie Magdelene LeBlanc	Simon, & Isabel Le Blanc	Oct. 25
Marie Magdelene Landry	Marin, & Pelagie Landry	Oct. 30
Charles Lincour	Charles, & Marie Babin	Nov. 4
Jean Louis Babin	Joseph, & Marie Landry	Nov. 17
Mar. Felicite LeBlanc	Isaac, & Marie Rose Melancon	Nov. 23
Paul Foret	Paul, & Marguerite Orillion	Nov. 23
Anne Felicite Landry	Olivier, & Marie Magdelene Hebert	Nov. 28
Joseph Landry	Simon, & Marguerite Babin	Dec. 1
Angelique Broussard	Simon, & Marguerite Blanchard	Dec. 12
Francoise Landry	Hyacinthe, & Marguerite Landry	Dec. 16
Michel Dugas	Francois, & Marguerite Babin	Dec. 25
Anne Hebert	Prosper, & Marie Dupuy	Dec. 27
Gregoire Landry	Paul Marie, & Bright Babin	Dec. 27
Joseph Buenventura	Franco, & Marie Louise Masson	Dec. 28

1776

Name	Parents	Date of birth
Paul Hilaire Le Blanc	Silvin, & Marie Babin	Jan. 14
Francois Roger	Joseph, & Anastasie Dugas	Feb. 13
Louis Landry	Joseph & Isabel Le Blanc	May 12
Marie Angele Landry	Maturin, & Anne Landry	May 13
Marie Joseph Dugas	Jean, & Anne LeBlanc	May 16
Helena Prejean	Aman, & Marie Therriot	June 14
Marguerite Landry	Vincent, & Suzanne Gaudin	July 4
Desire Valentin Richard	Aman, & Marie Anne Braud	Aug. 31
Etienne Braud	Paul, & Marie Marthe LeBlanc	Nov. 4
Narcisse Hebert	Etienne, & Anne Landry	11-7-78
Pierre Firmin Babin	Firmin, & Bibiana Braud	Dec. 6
Jean Gallien	Joseph, & Marie Bouton	Dec. 28

1777

Name	Parents	Date of birth
Marie Constance Lincour	Charles, & Marie Babin	9-17-78
Henriette Elisa Landry	Pierre, & Marguerite Allain	9-13-78
Charles Babin	Joseph, & Marine Le Blanc	May 12
Joseph Landry	Vincent, & Suzanne Gaudin	Sept. 21
Pannis Rothi	William, & Maniaue (St. Gabriel)	Nov. 18
Rosa Landry	Simon, & Anne Landry	Dec. 20
(Illegible) Hebert	Etienne, & Anne Landry	Dec. 28

1778

Name	Parents	Date of birth
Louis Aigu	Lorenzo, & Anne Roche, (St. Gabriel)	Jan. 4
Joseph Xaucry Richard	Paul, & Magdelene Martha Babin	Jan. 5
Jean Baptiste Le Blanc	Isaac, & Marie Melancon	July 1
Collet Hebert	Francois, & Marie Hebert	Aug. 13
Marie Barrett	William, & Francoise Lemoine	Aug. 16
Joseph Dugas	Athanas, & Rose Le Blanc	Sept. 3
Euphrosine Lanoux	Pierre, & Catherine LeBlanc	Sept. 7

Name	Parents	Date of birth
Hypolite Armand Braud	Paul, & Marie Marthe Le Blanc	Sept. 14
Marie Theotiste Landry	Olivier, & Marie Magdelene Hebert	Sept. 14
Jerome Gautreau	Aman, & Marie Landry	Sept. 21
Ann Catherine Le Blanc	Etienne, & Osite Le Blanc	Sept. 25
Magdelene Angelic Foret	Paul, & Marguerite Orillion	Nov. 10
Allain Landry	Pierre, & Marguerite Allain	Oct. 18
Poulonne Dugas	Francois, & Marguerite Babin	Oct. 24
Constance Duhon	Francois, & Eliabeth Landry	Nov. 5
Augustin Babin	Joseph, & Marie Landry	Nov. 27
Osite Victorin Landry	Joseph, & Osite Landry	Dec. 1
Eloy Babin	Jean Jacque, & Marguerite Landry	Dec. 1
Martha Landry	Joseph, & Magdeleine LeBlanc	Dec. 3
Marie Barbara Gallein	Joseph, & Marie Bouton	Dec. 4
Adeline Francoise Hamilton	Joseph, & Anastasie ————	Dec. 18
Paul Foret	Anselm, & Magdelene Le Blanc	Dec. 24

1779

Name	Parents	Date of birth
Jacque Landry	Jacque, & Francoise Blanchard	Jan. 1
Simon Broussard	Firmin, & Marie Magdelene Landry	Jan. 1
Celeste Landry	Charles, & Marie Babin	Jan. 3
Marie Celeste Dugas	Michel, & Sophie Forest	Jan. 7
Marguerite Pelagie Dugas	Michel, & Sophie Forest	Jan. 7
Anna Machet Foret	Pierre, & Marie Braud	Feb. 13
Francois Louis Benoit	Etienne, & Magdeleine Braud	Mar. 2
Joseph Alex. Babin	Efreme, & Marguerite Le Blanc	Mar. 19
Marie Babin	Charles, & Magdelena ————	Mar. 24
Marie Francoise Landry	Augustin, & Marie Foret	Mar. 30
Victor Dugas	Charles, & Rose Babin	Apr. 10
Juan Perez	Antonio, & Francisca Gonzales	Apr. 25
Pierre Vital Comes	Joseph, & Anna Landry	Apr. 28
Pierre Babin	Joseph, & Ositte Le Blanc	Apr. 30
Sabastian Juan Ruano	Alonzo, & Ygnacio de Betancores	May 20
Maria Antonia Cabellos	Domingo, & Rita Ferran	June 27
Marguerite Celeste Landry	Joseph, & Magdeline Foret	June 29
Marguerite Babin	Aman, & Anastasie Landry	Aug. 11
Angelena Mar. Melàncon	Joseph, & Barbara Babin	Sept. 14
Eloy Landry	Etienne, & Brigitte Trahan	Sept. 25
Francois Landry	Joseph, & Anna Granger	Oct. 5
Marguerite Joseph Godin	Charles, & Marie Babin	Oct. 13
Firmin Landry	Simon, & Marguerite Babin	Nov. 10
Anselmo Falcon	Gaspar, & Francisca Denez	Nov. 17
Susana Bonaventure	Francisco, & Maria L. Masson	Dec. 3
Angela Le Blanc	Silvain, & Marie Joseph Babin	Dec. 24

1780

Name	Parents	Date of birth
Jeanne Carmela Landry	Joseph, & Anna Bujol	Jan. 23
Marguerite Le Blanc	Simon, & Isabel Le Blanc	Jan. 25
Marie Magdeline Dugas	Athanas, & Rosa LeBlanc	Feb. 27
Anna Josefa Dugas	Athanas, & Rosa LeBlanc	Feb. 27
Madeleine Landry Babin	Joseph, & Marie Landry	Mar. 12
Francoise Le Blanc	Isaac, & Marie Melancon	Mar. 13

Name	Parents	Date of birth
Joseph Thadeo Landry	Joseph, & Marie Madeline LeBlanc	Mar. 18
Joseph Lacroix	Pierre, & Marguerite Mollere	Apr. 1
Henrietta Broussard	Firmin, & Madeleine Landry	Apr. 4
Martin Franco Aleman	Francisco, & Tomassa Bordon	June 3
Juan Rodriguez	Juan, & Josefa de'Orta	June 4
Pierre Augustine Landry	Pierre, & Marguerite Allain	July 4
Marguerite Babin	Joseph, & Ositte Le Blanc	July 15
Anastasie Dugas	Charles, & Rosa Babin	July 27
Edouard Landry	Joseph, & Marie Osite Landry	Aug. 21
Louis Hebert	Joseph, & Anastasie Landry	Aug. 25
Marguerite Bergeron	Charles, & Marie Foret	Aug. 27
Jeanne O'Brien	William, & Marie Noix	Sept. 22
Osite Barbe Melancon	Joseph, & Barbara Babin	Oct. 4
Jean Hubert Presse	Jean, of Ouachita, & Francoise Fogie	Nov. 5
Louis Chauvin	Jean Baptiste, & Anna Hernandez	Nov. 29
Victoria (illegible)	(Illegible)	Dec. 2
Franco (illegible)	(Illegible)	Dec. 2
Nicolas Doncel	Pierre, & Juana Ximenez	Nov. 30
Augustin Foret	Anselm, & Madeleine Le Blanc	Dec. 6

1781

Name	Parents	Date of birth
Marie Bacheron	Albert, & Marie Louise Pijon	Jan. 11
Joseph Gallien	Joseph, & Marie Bouton	Jan. 15
Michel Edward Dugas	Michel, & Sophie Foret	Jan. 17
Marie Anna Braud	Armand, & Marie Magdeline Clouatre	Jan. 17
Henrietta Bergeron	Jean Baptiste, & Marie Babin	Jan. 17
Landry Duhon	Francois, & Isabel Landry	Feb. 13
Marie Celeste Landry	Joseph, & Anna Bujol	Mar. 5
Louis Judice	Louis Judice, & Marguerita Paten	Feb. 15
Henry Landry	Olivier, & Marie Magdelene Hebert	Mar. 25
Mathilde Landry	Charles, & Anna Marie Babin	Apr. 18
Augustin Babin	Aman, & Anastasie Landry	Apr. 18
Marie Celeste Babin	Jean Jacque, & Marguerite Landry	June 14
Simon Le Blanc	Simon, & Isabel Le Blanc	June 24
Julienne Babin	Joseph, & Marie Landry (St. James)	July 18
Anna Victoria Landry	Vincent, & Susanne Gaudin	Aug. 9
Madleine Landry	Joseph, & Anna Grange	Aug. 18
Anna Henrietta Hebert	Prosper, & Marie Dupuis	Sept. 19
Henrietta Braud	Paul, & Marie Marthe Le Blanc	Sept. 19
Marine Braud	Paul, & Marie Marthe Le Blanc	Sept. 19
Henrietta Dugas	Athanas, & Rosa Le Blanc	Oct. 27
Henrietta Landry	Pierre, & Marie Landry	Oct. 31
Jean Presse	Jean, & Francoise Fogle	Nov. 5
Henrietta Melancon	Jacque, & Isabel Landry	Nov. 10
Marie Elise Melancon	Charles, & Felicite Landry	Nov. 11
Marie Magd. Broussard	Firmin, & Marie Magdeleine Landry	Nov. 12
Marie Le Blanc	Silvain, & Marie Joseph Babin	Nov. 12
Simon Babin	Efrem, & Marguerite Le Blanc	Dec. 27

Name	Parents	Date of birth
		1782
Anna Madeleine Landry	Etienne, & Bridget Trahan	Jan. 14
Joseph Desire Landry	Jacque, & Francoise Blanchard	Jan. 17
John Jones	Evan, & Marie Verret	Jan. 18
Nicolas Landry	Simon, & Anna Marguerite Babin	Feb. 15
Marie Louise La Croix	Pierre, & Marguerite Mollere	Mar. 22
Marie Magdelene Jealdre	Jacque, & Barbara Petit	Apr. 7
Simon Landry	Joseph, & Magdeleine Le Blanc	Apr. 15
Louis Foret	Paul, & Marguerite Orillion	May 28
Madelene Bonaventura	Francois, & Marie Louise Masson	Mar. 8
Marguerite Landry	Joseph, & Osite Landry	July 31
Juan Landry Vives	Don Juan, & Marguerite Bujol	Aug. —
Francoise	(illegible)	Aug. 15
Marie Elise Landry	Joseph, & Madeleine Babin	Sept. 30
Marie Carmen Ramirez	Ignacio, & Maria Santos Diaz	Oct. 14
Madeleine Gaudin	Charles, & Marie Joseph Babin	Oct. 20
Marie Celeste Le Blanc	Etienne, & Osite Le Blanc	Nov. 14
Pierre Gregoire Landry	Pierre, & Marguerite Allain	Nov. 17
Landry Babin	Aman, & Anastasie Landry	Nov. 30
Louisa Cantrelle	Jacques, & Dona Louisa	Dec. 3
Simon Theodore Babin	Firmin, & Isabel Brousse	Dec. 14
Francois Thom. Broussard	Firmin, & Magdeleine Landry	Dec. 21
Marie Celeste Landry	Joseph, & Anna Bujol	Dec. 27
		1783
Francois Duhon	Francois, & Isabel Landry	Jan. 15
Julie Clothilde Dugas	Michel, & Sofie Foret	Feb. 6
Dorothy Marron	Franco, & Isabel La Marthe	Feb. 12
Narcisse Le Blanc	Pierre, & Marguerite Braud	Mar. 14
Pierre Le Blanc	Isaac, & Marguérite Babin	May 9
Isabel	————, & Francisca Scrantin	May 26
Marie Magdelene Melancon	Charles, & Felicite Landry	June 17
Marie Angele Dugas	Charles, & Rosa Babin	Aug. 2
Marie Anna Bergeron	Charles, & Marie Forest	Aug. 20
Maria Rodriguez	Juan, & Josefa de Orta	Aug. 24
Adelaide Babin	Joseph, & Osite Le Blanc	Sept. 1
Louis Le Blanc	Simon, & Isabel Le Blanc	Sept. 29
Simon Pierre Le Blanc	Silvain, & Marie Joseph Babin	Oct. 20
Mariana Henrietta Landry	Pierre, & Marie Joseph Landry	Oct. 23
Simon Dubec	Pierre, & Pelagie Dome	Nov. 25
Jacque Firmin Hebert	Prosper, & Marie Dupuy	Mar. 2
Marie Marguerite Braud	Paul, & Isabel Babin	Dec. 11
Donate Landry	Jacque, & Francoise Blanchard	Nov. 12
Victor Martin Landry	Jacque, & Francoise Blanchard	Nov. 12
Juana Maria Buano	Alonzo, & Isabel Luxon	Nov. 3
Alexandre Hebert	Joseph, & Anastasie Landry	Nov. 21
Catalina Marie Bermudez	Manuel, & Maria Mossuma	Nov. 28
Marie Conception Lopez	Juan, & Maria Romano	Nov. 29
Jean Dugas	Francois, & Marguerite Babin	Nov. 29
Joseph Roger Dugas	Francois, & Marguerite Babin	Nov. 29

Name	Parents	Date of birth
Jacque Alexandre Babin	Jacque, & Margerita————	Dec. 1
Jacque Donate Landry	Joseph, & Madeleine Le Blanc	Dec. 11
Franco Antonio Navarro	Pablo, & Martha Acosta	Dec. 20
Augustin Broussard	Firmin, & Magdelene Landry	Dec. 20

1784

Name	Parents	Date of birth
Jose Antonio Hidalgo	Jose, & Isabel Morales	Jan. 6
Osite Barbe Mollere	Joseph, & Osite Barbe Blanchard	Jan. 8
Francois Achille Foret	Paul, & Marguerite Orillion	Feb. 7
Antoine Riviere	Bernard, & Maria Antonia de Orta	Feb. 24
Louise Babin	Joseph, & Marie Landry	Feb. 28
Jean Baptiste Terrio	Jean Baptiste, & Marguerite Hebert	Mar. 3
(illegible) Foret	Paul, & Marguerite Orillion	Mar. 11
Antonio Dominguez	Augustin, & Lorenzo Corbo	Mar. 29
Mathurin Landry	Etienne, & Brigitte Trahan	Mar. 31
Anna Marguerite Vives	Juan, & Marguerite Bujol	Apr. 8
Bernardo Antonio Morrino	Mathias, & Antonia Deniz	Apr. 12
Francesca Aug. Dominguez	Antonia, & Maria Franqucz	Apr. 12
Antoine Lorenzo Doucet	Manuel, & Catalina Ximenez	Apr. 13
Antonio Joseph Diaz	Antonio, & Maria C. Truxillo	Apr. 15
Francois Godin	Charles, & Marie Babin	Jan. 12
Maria Teresa Hernandez	Estevan, & Isabel Rodriguez	May 20
Anna Constance Esteve	Domingo, & Isabel Lancia	July 26
Joseph Garcia	Josef, & Barbara Diez	Aug. 5
Marie Louise Dugas	Michel, & Sophie Foret	Aug. 20
Jacque Leconte	Jacque, & Marie Marthe Le Blanc	Aug. 25
Catalina Con. Hernandez	Lorenzo, & Maria Ximenez	Sept. 5
Pierre La Croix	Pierre, & Marguerite Mollere	Sept. 13
Louise Con. Hernandez	Bartholome, & Isabel Hidalgo	Sept. 25
Pierre Babin	Aman, & Anna Anastasie Landry	Nov. 4
Alex. Joseph Braud	Pierre, & Brigitte Forest	Dec. 12

1785

Name	Parents	Date of birth
Henrietta Babin	Joseph, & Ozitte Le Blanc	Jan. 18
Marie Rose Le Blanc	Mathurin, & Rosalie Terrio	Jan. 6
Francois Babin	Firmin, & Isabel Babin	Mar. 13
Joseph Mollere	Joseph, & Ozitte Blanchard	May 25
Oliver Pierre Melancon	Charles, & Felicie Landry	July 5
Anaclet Braud	Paul, & Isabel Babin	July 13
Firmin Broussard	Firmin, & Magdeleine Landry	July 16
Nanet Nassant	Joseph, & Marguerite Landry	July 26
Charlotte Marie Le Blanc	Olivier, & Marie Magdeleine Luves	Oct. 4
Clara Adelaide Como	Benoit, & Anna Blanchard	Sept. 15
Magdeleine Le Blanc	Isaac, & Marguerite Babin	Nov. 12
Paul Dugas	Charles, & Rose Duhon	Nov. 24
Celeste Pitre	Ambrose, & Isabel Dugas	Dec. 4
Joseph Le Blanc	Joseph, & Marguerite Foret	Dec. 13
Ositte Le Blanc	Isaac, & Marguerite Babin	Dec. 13
Pierre Landry	Joseph, & Magdeleine Babin	Dec. 24

1786

Name	Parents	Date of birth
Thomas Gonzales	Pedro Manuel, & Juana Ximenez	Jan. 2
Marie Cavalier	Pedro, & Maria Gonzalcs	Jan. 4

Name	Parents	Date of birth
Marie Clara Vives	Don Juan, & Marguerite Bujol	Jan. 20
Carlos Bergeron	Charles, & Marie Foret	Jan. 22
Reynaldo Landry	Enselm, & Francoise Blanchard	Jan. 22
Marie Magdeleine Dugas	Jacque, & Marie Dugas	Jan. 25
Louis Babin	Aman, & Anastasie Landry	Jan. 26
Nicolas Ivan Rousseau	Ivan, & Anna Thibodaux	Feb. 1
Marguerite Le Blanc	Silvain, & Josepha Babin	Feb. 1
Jean Marie Sanbourg	Cecelio, & Catalina Dio	Feb. 2
Nicolas Liret	Jean, & Marie Magdelene Sanbourg	Feb. 5
Simon Boudreaux	Joseph, & Marguerite Richard	Feb. 12
Pedro Kerne	Lorenzo, & Marie (illegible)	Feb. 15
Maria Dominguez	Antonio, & Marie Franquez	Feb. 17
Marie Carmen Ruano	Alonzo, & Isabel Luccan	Feb. 18
Elie Gautreau	Marion, & Gertrude Bourg	Feb. 19
Joseph Gautreau	Marion, & Gertrude Bourg	Feb. 19
Baltazar Le Blanc	Simon, & Isabelle Le Blanc	Feb. 19
Henrietta Adelaide Landry	Pierre, & Marguerite Allain	Feb. 19
Jacque Dupuis	Pierre, & Marie Dupuis	Feb. 28
Nicolas Verret	Nicolas, & Marguerite Ostroye	Mar. 2
(illegible) Dufresne	Charles, & Marie Ada	Apr. 4
Joseph Cherami	Joseph, & Anna Aucoin	Apr. 17
Catherine Arabi	Joseph, & Rita Perez	Apr. 15
Ana Antonia Diez	Antonio, & Maria Conception	Apr. 18
Lucia Blanchard	Firmin, & Madeleine Bujol	May 21
Ysabel Antonia Rodriguez	Franco Ant., & Ysabel de Orta	May 18
Antonio Alleman	Franco, & Thomassa Giroire	May 30
Andrea Dominguez	Augustin, & Lorenza Corbo	Aug. 2
Marie Comes	Joseph, & Anna Landry	Aug. 13
Joseph Marie Ordonez	Manuel, & Marianna Doublin	Aug. 21
Maria Rodriguez	Juan, & Josefa de Orta	Aug. 28
Maria Luisa Pineta	Louis, & Maria Le Blanc	Oct. 1
Marie Jeanne Landry	Etienne, & Brigitte Trahan	Oct. 8
Joseph Landry	Joseph, & Anna Bujol	Oct. —
Nicolas Pierre Currel	Jean Pierre, & Marie Hebert	Nov. 17
Julia Condule Dugas	Athanas, & Rose Le Blanc	Nov. 17
Marie Acosta	Domingo, & Marcelena Truxillo	Dec. 7
Michel Aucoin	Michel, & Rose Laforest	Dec. —
Marguerita Dugas	Francois, & Marguerite Babin	Dec. 8
Augustina Falcon	Christobal, & Josefa Ruiz	Dec. 8

1787

Name	Parents	Date of birth
Magdelena M. Montesino	Juan Josef, & Maria Navarrez	Jan. 1
Marie Modeste Guedry	Firmin, & Marguerite Landry	Jan. —
Anna Marie Dubois	Jacque, & Marie Michel	Jan. 4
Constance Dugas	Ambrose, & Marie Pitre	Feb. 4
Marie Dupuy	Etienne, & Marie Dugas	Feb. 4
Marie Anna Cheben	Jerome, & Marie Pitre	Feb. 14
Lawrence Boudreaux	Jean Baptiste, & Marguerite Dorel	Feb. 17
Godefroy Verret	(Illegible)	Feb. 18
Mathias Bermudez	Manuel, & Maria Antonia Monson	Feb. 26
Felicite Sonnier	Jean Baptiste, & Maria Antoinette (Illegible)	Mar. 9

Name	Parents	Date of birth
Mannette Daigle	Jean Baptiste, & Marg'te. Simoneaux	Mar. 11
Charles Braud	Paul, & Isabel Babin	Mar. 11
Alexandre Simoneaux	Simon, & Isabel Daigle	Mar. 9
Francisco Ourso	Martin, Catalina Marrero	Mar. 9
Marie Madeline Bourg	Pierre, & Marie Bujol	Mar. 25
Belloni Charles Forest	Charles, & Margie Magelin Blanchard	Apr. 8
Juana Marie Aleman	Antonio, & Marie Plasencia	Apr. 8
Francisco Licord	Juan, & Marie Braud	Apr. 16
Oliver Sormaro	Louis, & Anna Trahan	Apr. 17
Pierre Caussin	Pierre, & Marg'te, Landry	Apr. 22
Marie Magdeline Lincour	Charles, & Osite Landry	Apr. 24
Joseph Dugas	Joseph, & Sophie Forest	Apr. 29
Jacque Terrio	Jacque, & Francisca Cheven	Apr. 8
Marguerite Louise Landry	Pierre, & Marie Landry	Apr. 7
Victoria Guedry	Joseph, & Magdeline Como	Apr. 7
Constance Simoneaux	Joseph, & Magdelien Bourg	Apr. 7
Fabien Guillot	Fabien, & Anna Gouraux	May 17
Isidore Martinez	Franco, & Marie Antonia Ximenez	May 18
Isabel Kling	Henry, & Catherine Lambert	May 20
Joseph Le Blanc	Alexandre, & Anna Trahan	May 22
Simon Babin	Joseph, & Osite Le Blanc	May 27
Marie Daigle	Jean, & Marie Dugas	May 27
Rose Anna Boudreaux	Joseph, & Rosa Gautreaux	May 30
Jeanne Adel'de Boudreaux	Joseph, & Rosa Gautreaux	May 30
Marie Acosta	Lorenzo, & Juana Hernandez	June 24
Juan Mathias Plasencia	Juan, & Marie Franca Borgez	June 24
Marie Tircuit	Francois, & Barbe Bursua	July 11
Juan Josef Rodriguez	Franco Antonio, & Isabel Orta	July 13
Marie Isabel Melancon	Charles, & Felicite Landry	Aug. 2
Marie Terrio	Jean, & Marie Mag. Landry	Aug. 11
Maria Zauallas	Domingo, & Rita Ferron	Aug. 13
Bartholemew E. Le Blanc	Isaac, & Marguerite Babin	Aug. 18
Isabel Landry	Jean Pierre, & Isabel Guieron	Aug. 25
Josefa Hernandez	Josef, & Maria la Riz	Aug. 30
Marie Juncal (?)	Louis, & Marie Rose Dugas	Sept. —
Maria Marguerita Vega	Andres, & Constancia Luson	Sept. 2
Laurent Blanchard	Laurent, & Anna Hebert	Sept. 2
Marie Anna Trahan	Maturin, & Marie Blanchard	Sept. 2
Santiago Navarro	Paul, & Maria Acosta	Sept. 20
Marguerite Dugas	Pierre, & Rose LeBlanc	Sept. 24
Isabel Anna Doucet	Pierre, & Juana Ximenez	Oct. 5
(illegible) Riviere	Yves, & Anna Thibodaux	Oct. 5
Joseph Sylvestre Bujol	Jean, & Marie Bourg	Oct. 8
Maria Rosalia Hernandez	Estevan, & Isabel Rodriguez	Oct. 9
Maria Madeleine Landry	Charles, & Marie Babin	Oct. 14
Antonio Josef Maxent	Antonio, & Marie Pitre	Oct. 14
Felipa Antonia Franco	Fernando, & Maria Perera	Oct. 20
Pedro Sanchez	Pedro, & Maria Hernandez	Oct. 25
Maria Le Blanc	Vincent, & Barbara Diez	Oct. 25

Name	Parents	Date of birth
Marie Dolores Mollere	Joseph, & Barbara Osite Blanchard	Nov. 1
Antonio Escano	Domingo, & Juana Rodriguez	Nov. 4
Rene Dugas	Theodore, & Victoria Foret	Nov. 6
Modeste Pinette	Louis, & Marie Vincent	Nov. 6
Lorenzo Dugas	Charles, & Rose Babin	Nov. 18
Joseph Orternz	Lorenzo, & Maria Ximenez	Dec. 8
Isabel Babin	Firmin, & Isabel Braud	Dec. 25
Jean Baptiste Bourg	Fabian, & Marie Boudreaux	Dec. 25
Anna Constance Liret	Jean, & Magdelene Daranbourg	Dec. 31

1788

Name	Parents	Date of birth
Marie Magdelene Hebert	Joseph, & Fant Duransbourg	Jan. 1
Marie Magdeleine Duhon	Jacque, & Anna Braud	Jan. 1
Silvestre Martin	Antonio, & Paula Morrina	Jan. 6
Josef Antonio Acosta	Juan, & Theresa Corbo	Jan. 23
Rene Marie Landry	Pierre, & Marguerite Allain	Jan. 27
Isabel Landry	Joseph, & Osite Landry	Feb. 17
Jean Francois Gautreau	Jean, & Francoise Blanchard	Feb. 17
Jean Joseph LeJeune	Joseph, & Marie Adelaide Landry	Feb. 17
Domingo Truxillo	Antonio, & Maria Dominguez	Feb. 21
Pierre Melancon	Joseph, & Marguerite Landry	Mar. 3
Lorenzo Dominguez	Augustin, & Lorenza Corbo	Mar. 3
Jose Maria Ordonez	Manuel, & Marianna Doublin	Mar. 24
Isabel Babin	Aman, & Anastasie Landry	Mar. 24
Etienne Dupuis	Etienne, & Osite Dugas	Mar. 24
Timothy Hebert	Isaac, & Marie Daigle	Mar. 24
Manuel Barrios	Manuel, & Antonia Rodriguez	Mar. 25
Christobal Acosta	Domingo, & Marcelline Truxillo	Apr. 6
Theresa Diaz	Josef, & Maria Corbo	Apr. 6
Valentin Theriot	Olivier, & Marie Aucoin	May 1
Marie Madeleine Landry	Joseph Athanas, & Magdelene Babin	May 1
Rene Landry	Pierre, & Marguerite Allain	Dec. 8
Marie Bourg	Jean, & Catherine Bujol	May 4
Maturin Chevalier	Maturin, & Francoise Pitre	May 5
Clarice Landry	Paul, & Francoise Hebert	May 12
Jean Baptiste Guillot	Fabian, & Anna Quirina	May 12
Marie Naquin	Joseph, & Marie Arsement	May 12
Anna Landry	Anselm, & Francoise Blanchard	June 12
Ritco Cabellero	Pedro, & Maria Granco	June 14
Constance Gomez	Joseph, & Anna Landry	June 21
Jean Baptiste Guedry	Firmin, & Marguerite Landry	June 22
Mariana Le Blanc	Moyse, & Marie Magdelene Bertand	July 1
Marie Joseph Dugas	Ambroise, & Marie Pitre	July 6
Francois Riviere	Bernard, & Antonia de Orta	July 19
Domingo Rodriguez	Juan, & Josefa de Orta	July 19
Maria Manuela Gomez	Angel, & Lazara Padilla	July 22
Gregoire Le Blanc	Enselm, & Marie Magdeleine Babin	May 27
Clarice Trahan	Pierre, Maria Clemence	May 27
Celeste Le Blanc	Simon, & Isabel Le Blanc	May 27
Manuel Esteves	Domingo, & Isabel Garcia	May 27
Baptiste Alberton	Augustin, & Marie Goyette	May 27

Name	Parents	Date of birth
Jean Braud	Pierre, & Brigit Forest	May 27
Marie Verret	Philip, & Marie Hebert	Aug. 21
Rosalia Falcon	Gaspar, & Francesca Mateo	Aug. 31
Juan Acosta	Andres, & Josefa de Orta	Sept. 7
Anna Landry	Jean Athanas, & Anna Murey	Sept. 15
Marie Magdeleine Dugas	Simon, & Genevieve Bourg	Sept. 14
Marie Clara Daigle	Jean, & Marguerite Simoneaux	Sept. 21
Joseph Comes	Joseph, & Anna Landry	Sept. 21
Pierre Braud	Paul, & Isabel Babin	Oct. 3
Desire Le Blanc	Gregoire, & Barbe Babin	Oct. 18
Jean Baptiste Robichaux	Jean Baptiste, & Martha Le Blanc	Oct. 24
Etienne Robichaux	Henry, & Magdelene Le Blanc	Oct. 24
Rafael Bourin	Philip, & Brigit Trahan	Oct. 27
Marie Richard	Charles, & Marie Joseph Trahan	Nov. 2
Jean Baptiste Bergeron	Charles, & Marie Forrest	Nov. 16
Marie Clemence Simoneaux	Simon, & Isabel Daigle	Nov. 23
Marie Louise Dugas	Athanas, & Rose Le Blanc	Dec. 7
Joseph Dubois	Jacque, & Marie Michel	Dec. 9
Maria Dominguez	Antonio, & Maria Franquez	Dec. 11
Nicolas Bermudez	Manuel, & ———— Perez	Dec. 13
Marie Michel	Joseph, & Marie Le Blanc	Dec. 14
Louis Francois Dantin	Louis, & Marguerite Braud	Dec. 25

1789

Name	Parents	Date of birth
Louis Juncal	Louis, & Marie Dugas	Jan. 25
Antonio Guilfaux	Jean, & Eleonore Plasencia	Jan. 29
Marie Rousseau	Jacque, & Charlotte Oubre	Feb. 15
Charles Boudreau	Etienne, & Victoire Gautreau	Feb. 24
Balthazar Franco	Louis, & Sebastiana Aleman	Mar. 20
Felicite Dugas	Michel, & Sophie Foret	Mar. 22
Luis Antonio Martinez	Franco, & Maria Antonia Ximenez	Mar. 23
Manuel Morrina	Mathias, & Antonia Martin	Mar. 28
Marie Forgeron	Joseph, & Marie Boudreaux	Apr. 14

NOTE: No doubt there were quite a number of others who were born in Ascension Parish, Louisiana, during the aforesaid, of whose birth no record is in existence. In numerous cases above the date of Baptism is given. Slaves were born in Ascension parish as follows: 1773—3, 1775—3, 1778—2; 1779—9; 1780—1; 1781—1; 1782—1; 1784 ——30; 1785—5; 1786—10; 1788—1. Of course, there were others, but of them no record is found.

Statistics on Pioneer Days

Year	Births	Marriages	Deaths	Year	Births	Marriages	Deaths
1772	19	7	8	1805	0	14	21
1773	25	8	4	1806	0	20	17
1774	30	9	3	1807		19	36
1775	35	14	11	1808		19	28
1776	12	4	7	1809		25	32
1777	7	0	4	1810		21	28
1778	22	3	0	1811		15	40
1779	26	8	32	1812		8	39
1780	25	2	14	1813		5	14
1781	27	6	7	1814		2	14
1782	22	11	9	1815		5	21
1783	29	9	15	1816		15	20
1784	25	11	3	1817		19	20
1785	16	1	8	1818		9	12
1786	41	41	23	1819		12	49
1787	68	23	3	1820		11	23
1788	62	18	13	1821		16	15
1789	9	23	13	1822		16	61
1790		16	17	1823		10	66
1791		17	14	1824		12	46
1792		22	15	1825		18	31
1793		17	9	1826		21	50
1794		7	13	1827		31	35
1795		9	15	1828		13	59
1796		9	10	1829		12	41
1797		11	19	1830			43
1798		4	13	1831			64
1799		10	13	1832			65
1800		9	15	1833			98
1801		11	7	1834			80
1802		17	15	1835			67
1803		7	26	1836			75
1804		10	15	1837			49
				1838			43
				1839			65
				1840			81
				1841 to 11-5-4			53

Note: As shown by the records of Ascension Catholic Church, Donaldsonville, La., which was established on Aug. 15, 1772. The records indicate that no marriages were performed between June, 1776, and Oct. 1778. Total marriages performed at Ascension Church between 1772 and 1829 were 740. Births for omitted years not obtained. The census of 1788 gave the district of Lafourche (now Ascension parish) a population of 1,164, while in 1785 showed only 646 inhabitants. We find that approximately 500 Acadian exiles settled in this area between 1785 and 1788.

Front entrance Court House, Donaldsonville, Louisiana. J. S. Barman and Mrs. L. P. Montgomery.

"Linwood" Ante-Bellum Home
of a Minor Family.

THE HUMBLE HOMES OF THE PIONEERS

THE first places of abode of the exiles have long since crumbled into dust. Almost one hundred seventy years have elapsed since the Acadians went forth into the dense forests of the Second Acadian settlement and there felled the mighty cypress trees. These trees they converted into posts, pickets, boards and other building material which they used to construct their small cottages. The reader must use his powers of imagination to recreate pictures of the humble homes of this gallant band of pioneers. Rough were the homes, but therein dwelt a people who lived at peace with their God and their fellow-man. At the beginning their houses were constructed without floors, other than the aluvial soil of this region. Split boards served as a roof, and split pickets covered the outer walls. All foundation material, as well as other heavy timbers, were hand-hewn and as "solid as a rock." Some of the old buildings, on being demolished a century afterwards, were found to contain material which was still in a good state of preservation. One may imagine the utter loneliness of the pioneers by reason of their isolation. The dwellings were far apart, and the settlers were completely out of touch with the surrounding regions. Neighbor told neighbor what he had heard, and thus news was transmitted from one to another. No mail, newspapers, telephone, roads, railroad or boat service! Indeed, they lived "far from the madding crowd's ignoble strife." The river—ever flowing towards the sea—was at their front door, and the pirogue was the only means of travel. A trip to the small town of New Orleans was an event of great importance in the life of any one so fortunate as to be able to make the journey. Upon returning from such a trip, the settler devoted considerable time to the matter of informing his neighbors what he had seen or learned. Very poor, they endured all manner of hardships, but, as the years passed, their homes and farms were improved. The more prosperous ones, after 1797, occasionally received "The Monitor of Louisiana"—the first newspaper published in New Orleans and Louisiana. In time some of the exiles built floors of pickets in their homes; then came small galleries, planked overhead. In time, we find them building their cottages "on blocks," or pillars, and the walls were filled with a mixture of mud and moss which was placed between the posts. The exiles called it "bousillier entre les poteaux." An idea of this type of construction may be obtained from the picture of the ruins of an old home in Brusly St. Martin, near Belle Rose, Louisiana, which is reproduced in another section of this book.

Brief descriptions of the early homes of the exiles were obtained from the office of the Honorable Henry A. Dugas, Recorder of the parish of Ascension, another descendant of the Acadian exiles. This data will give some idea as to dimensions, etc. Verbal descriptions were supplied by L. Bertin Duplessis, Louis L. LeBlanc, J. Yve Landry, John A. Marchand, Jr., F. Harold Marchand, L. E. Wright and J. Clarence Bouchereau. Abbreviations, signs and symbols used: ab., above; bel., below; gal., gallery. The original acts were found in the office of the recorder of conveyances of the parish of Ascension.

Settler	Home	Date
		1771
Etienne Le Blanc	House on ground, 20' x 14', front gal., surrounded, covered and floored with pickets	Nov. 27
Joseph Lincour	House of posts in ground, 30' x 11', surrounded and covered with pickets	Dec. 25
		1773
Joseph Prejean	House on ground, 22' x 16', mud-moss walls, surrounded with pickets	Dec. 26
		1774
Paul Melancon	House on ground, 28' x 16', planked above and below with pickets	Apr. 10
Etienne Landry	A small hut of piece on piece, covered with pickets	Aug. 4
Abram Landry	House on ground, 30' in length, surrounded and planked, above and below, with pickets	Nov. 2
		1775
Aman Prejean	House on ground, 26' x 17', mud-moss walls, surrounded with pickets, covered with boards, planked ab. and bel. with pickets	Jan. 22
Jean Baptiste Milhomme	House on ground, 28' x 16', surrounded, covered and planked, ab. and bel. with pickets	Feb. 17
Francois Mollere	House on ground, 23' x 15'	June 27
Charles Prejean	House on ground, 22' x 16', surrounded, covered and floored with pickets	Dec. 13
Aman Babin	House on ground, 30' x 16', surrounded, covered and floored, ab. and bel. with pickets	Dec. 14
		1776
Augustin Broussard	House on ground, 20' x 16', surrounded, covered and planked, ab. and bel. with pickets	May 14
Jean Baptiste Braud	Small house in ruins	May 27

Settler	Home	Date
Honore Vissaus	House on ground, 20' x 16', surrounded, covered and planked, ab. and bel. with pickets	Oct. 21
Pierre Bujol, dit	Storehouse of posts in ground, 16' x 18', surrounded and covered with pickets	Oct. 31
Jean Baptiste Chauvin ...	House of posts in ground, 25' x 15', gal. on both grande face, covered and floored, ab. and below with pickets.....	Nov. 4
Joseph Granger	House on ground, 20' x 13', surrounded, covered and floored with pickets	Nov. 6
Joseph Richard	House on ground, 21' x 14', surrounded, covered and planked, ab. and bel. with pickets	Nov. 8
Silvain Le Blanc	House on ground, 26' x 15', front gal., covered with boards, mud-moss walls	Nov. 7

1777

Claude Duhon	House on ground, 25' x 15', gal., surrounded with pickets, covered with boards	Jan. 2
Joseph Richard	Small house in ruins	Feb. 16
Amand Prejean	House on ground, 28' x 17', surrounded with pickets, covered with boards	May 19
Augustin Bujol	House on ground, 25' x 16', front gal., surrounded, covered and planked, above and below with pickets	Sept. 23
Basil Landry	House on ground, 21' x 14', surrounded, covered and planked, above and below, with pickets	Nov. 4
Desire Le Blanc	House on ground, 35' x 16', surrounded, covered and planked, ab. and bel., with pickets	Nov. 30

1778

Jacque Landry	House on ground, 20' x 15', front gal., surrounded, covered and floored with pickets	Feb. 5
Jean Duhon	House on ground, 24' x 15'	Mar. 25
Firmin Broussard	House on ground, 18' x 12', front gal., 4', surrounded, covered and floored with pickets	Apr. 4
Joseph Landry, dit Belle Homme	House on ground, 20' x 16', surrounded, covered and floored with pickets	Apr. 25
Mrs. Pierre Landry	House on ground, 38' x 16', covered with boards, surrounded and floored, ab. and bel. with pickets	May 17

1779

George Urquhart	House on ground, 42' x 15', front gal., surrounded and covered with pickets	Feb. 18

Settler	Home	Date
Thomas Topham	House on ground, 24′ x 15′, surrounded and covered with pickets	Apr. 12
Jean Baptiste Braud	House on ground, 26′ x 16′, surrounded and covered with pickets	Oct. 20
Joseph Godet	House on ground, 25′ x 15′, front gal., 6′ covered with boards, surrounded with pickets	Oct. 21

1780

Charles Babin	House on ground, 20′ x 10′, front gal., covered with boards, surrounded and floored with pickets	Mar. 31
Nicolas Doublin	House with posts in ground, 25′ x 15′, front and rear gal's., and mud-moss walls, covered and floored with pickets	Apr. 2
Enselme Belisle	House of posts in ground, 24′ x 16′, surrounded and covered with planks	Apr. 22
Pierre Landry	House on ground, 25′ x 16′	May 7
Jacque Cantrelle	House on ground, 29′ x 15′, with kitchen posts in ground, surrounded and covered with pickets	May 17
Charles Braud	House on ground, 20′ x 16′, surrounded, covered and floored with pickets	May 20
Simon Le Blanc	House on ground, 35′ x 16′, surrounded, covered and planked, ab. and bel. with pickets	Sept. 3
William O'Brien	House on ground, 20′ x 16′, surrounded, covered and floored, ab. and bel., with pickets	Oct. 4
Antoine Boisdore	House on ground, 22′ x 14′, surrounded, covered and planked, ab. and bel., with pickets, front gal. 6′	Nov. 27
Noel Perrett	House on ground, 25′ x 16′	Dec. 12
Maturin Le Blanc	House on ground, 22′ x 15′, kitchen of posts in ground, surrounded and covered with pickets	Dec. 12

1781

Rene Landry (Mrs.)	House on ground, 30′ x 18′	June 7
Etienne Bujol (Mrs.)	House on ground, 30′ x 16′, covered with boards and surrounded with pickets	Sept. 30
Chas. Babin	House on ground, 20′ x 10′, gal. 5′, covered with boards and surrounded and planked with pickets	Oct. 4

1782

Joseph Babin, dit Dios	House 20′, 6′ gal'y., covered with pickets, surrounded with pickets	May 7
Simon Landry	House on ground, 26′, mud-moss walls, covered with pickets	May 16

Settler	Home	Date
Isaac LeBlanc	House on ground, 30′ x 16′, front and rear gal's, mud-moss walls, planked and covered with boards .... May 13	
Mrs. Paul Braud	House on ground, 28′ x 16′, surrounded, covered and planked, ab. and bel., with pickets .... May 15	
Joseph Guedry	House on ground, 20′ x 12′, front and real gal. .... Dec. 10	
Olivier Landry	House on ground, 30′ x 12′, surrounded and covered with pickets ..... Dec. 21	

1783

Manuel Quintero	Small house on ground .... Jan. 2	
Pierre Belly	House of posts in ground, 48′ long. Mar. 17	
Enselme Blanchard	House on ground, 35′ x 16′, front and rear gals., mud-moss walls, planked ab. and bel., and covered with boards ... Mar. 25	
Charles Forrest	House on ground, 25′ x 16′, surrounded, covered and planked, ab. and bel., with pickets .... Mar. 29	

1784

Armand Braud	House on ground, 26′ x 16′, surrounded and covered with pickets ...... Feb. 6	
Joseph Landry, dit Dios ..	House on ground, 30′ long, surrounded and covered with pickets .... Mar. 3	
Jacque Le Conte	House on ground, 24′ x 15′, front gal., mud-moss walls .... July 6	
Francois Duhon	House on ground, 20′ x 15′, surrounded and covered with pickets ..... Aug. 10	
Jean Melancon	House on ground, 24′ x 15′, front gal., mud-moss walls .... Aug. 20	
Jacque Landry	House on ground, 30′ x 16′, front and real gal's, mud-moss walls, floored below with planks, ab. with pickets, covered in front with boards and in the rear with pickets .... Dec. 18	

1785

Charles Forrest	House on ground, 25′ x 16′, surrounded and covered with pickets ..... Apr. 10	
Joseph Landry, dit a Petit Abram	House on ground, 24′ x 16′, front and rear gal's., mud-moss walls, covered with boards .... Feb. 24	
Mrs. Mary O'Brian	House on ground, 20′ x 16′, front and rear gal's., mud-moss walls, planked ab. and bel., covered with pickets ..... Dec. 29	

1886

Jean Baptiste Chauvin ...	House on ground, 25′ x 16′, surrounded and covered with pickets ...... Feb. 25	
Amand Gautros	House on ground, 30′ x 16′, surrounded and covered with pickets ..... Mar. 11	

88

Settler	Home	Date
Pierre Landry, dit la veilliard	House on ground, 31' x 16', front gals. 6', surrounded with pickets, covered with boards	Oct. 14
Firmin Broussard	House on ground, 20' x 14', mud-moss walls, planked ab. and bel., covered with pickets	Nov. 22
Etienne Bujol	House on ground, 30' x 16', front and rear gal's., floored ab. & bel., surrounded with pickets, covered with boards....	Dec. 19

1787

Prosten Hebert	House on ground, 20' x 12', fr. and rear gal's., surrounded and covered with pickets	Jan. 3
Pierre Braud	House on ground, front gal., mud-moss walls	Jan. 24
Mathurin Le Blanc	House on ground, 23' x 15', surrounded and covered with pickets	Jan. 30
Etienne Landry, dit Le jeune	House on ground, 28' x 16', surrounded and covered with pickets	May 29
Firmin Dupuis	House on ground, 20' x 15', surrounded, covered and planked with pickets	Aug. 1
Charles Lincour	Small house of posts in ground	Aug. 6
Pierre Landry, fils	House on ground, 31' x 16', front gal., surrounded with pickets and covered with boards	Aug. 16
Lucas Morice	House of posts in ground	July 8
Pierre Carmouche	House on ground, 20' x 14', mud-moss walls, planked ab. and bel., covered with pickets	Nov. 6
Francois Carmouche	House on ground, same as above..	Nov. 6

1788

Charles Peytavin	House on ground, 20' x 16', mud-moss walls, covered with pickets, with gal's.	Nov. 20
Charles Forest	House on ground, 20' x 15', mud-moss walls, gal's. on both grande face, covered with pickets	Dec. 12

1789

Pierre Arceneaux	House of posts in ground, 12' x 20', covered with pickets	Jan. 2
Andre Dominic Rosignol	House on ground	Mar. 2
Jean Nic. Forcenal	House of posts in ground, 45' x 14', with galleries on both grande face ...	Sept. 7
Joseph Mollere	House of posts in ground	Dec. 7
Francois Duhon	House on ground, 20' x 16', mud-moss walls	Dec. 13
Mrs. Pierre Bourg	House on ground, 20' x 14', mud-moss walls, covered with pickets	Dec. 20

Settler	Home	Date
		1790
Joseph Bujol	House of posts in ground, 30' x 15', with gal's.	July 30
Antoine Maxent	House of posts in ground	Sept. 25
		1791
Jean Villeneuve	House on ground, 31' x 16'	Apr. 8
Jean Bujol	House on ground, 20' x 14', mud-moss walls, covered with pickets	May 20
Jacque Therriot	House on ground, 20' x 14'	Aug. 31
		1792
Vincent Landry	House on ground, 20' x 16', front gal., mud-moss walls, covered with pickets	Jan. 9
Anselm Le Blanc	House on ground, 21' x 14', gal'y., on each grande face, mud-moss walls, covered with pickets	Jan. 22
Etienne Landry	House on ground, 20' x 16', gal. around	Feb. 13
Pierre Bourg	House on ground, 20' x 14', mud-moss walls, covered with pickets	May 9
Michel Debergue	Cabin of posts in ground, surrounded and covered with pickets	Apr. 28
		1793
Louis Judice	House of posts in ground, 37' x 13', gal's., on both grande face	Jan. 10
Firmin Landry	House on ground, 20' x 16', gal's. on both fronts	Mar. 28
Joseph Guedry	Small house on ground	Dec. 20
		1794
Eusebe Arceneaux	House of posts in ground	Feb. 16
Charles Collier	Small house of posts in ground, gal's. on both grande face	Apr. 8
Isaac Le Blanc	House on ground, 30' x 16', 7' gal's. on both grande face	July 6
Jean Baptiste Robichaux	Small house on ground	Sept. 21
Jean Baptiste Pechoux	House 16' sq., gal. at both ends, covered with pickets	Oct. 5
Widow Isaac LeBlanc	House on ground, 24' x 16', gal. on each grande face	Oct. 25
Joseph Landry, dit Dios	House on ground, 30' x 16'	Nov. 30
		1795
Charles Bergeron	House on ground, front gal'y.	Jan. 3
Paul Braud	House on ground, 32' x 16', gal'y. on each end	Jan. 9
Jos. Dubourg LeBlanc	House of posts in ground, 20' x 14', gal'y. on each end	Mar. 12
Nicolas Doublin	House on ground, 20' x 14', mud-moss walls, front and end gal's., planked ab. and below	Aug. 1

Settler	Home	Date
		1796
Antonio Dias	House of posts in ground	Mar. 4
Francois Landry	House of posts in ground, 30' x 15', mud-moss walls, covered with pickets	June 18
Simon Landry	House on ground, 27' x 15', gal'y. on both grande face	Oct. 2
		1797
Jean Baptiste Gautreau	House on ground, 18' x 16', gal. on both grande face	Mar. 13
Louis Robichaux	House on ground, 20' x 15'	Apr. 22
Henry Kling	House on ground, 20' x 15', kitchen of posts in ground	Aug. 16
		1798
Louis Mollere	House on ground, 20' x 15', gal'y. front and rear	Mar. 27
Joseph Bertoniere	House on ground, 20' x 17', front and rear galleries	Aug. 25
Joseph Bujol	House on ground, 30' x 15', front and rear galleries	Sept. 1
		1799
Manuel Romano	House, 20' x 12'	Jan. 10
		1800
Paul Forest	House, 22' x 15'	Jan. 16
Charles Melancon	House, 20' x 15'	Mar. 6
Joachim Marroy	House, 20'	Mar. 27
Bartolo Hernandez	House, 20' of posts in ground	May 31
Enselme Forest	House, 25' x 15', with gallery	June 21
Michel Dugas	House, 20' x 15'	July 11
Olivier Landry	House, 20' x 15'	July 5
Alexandre Dupre	House, 25' long	Aug. 20
Joseph Mollere	House on ground, 48' x 16'	Sept. 26
Louis Judice	House on ground, 27' x 16'	Sept. 30
		1801
Raymond Braud	House on blocks	Jan. 15
Enselm Le Blanc	House, 20' x 12'	Mar. 5
Dominic Bourgeois	House of posts in ground, 25' x 15'	May 6
Joseph Comes	House, 26' x 16', built on blocks	May 21
Michel Manuel Dugas	New house, 22' x 16', of posts in ground	May 21
Paul Braud	House, 31' x 15', new, with gal's	Sept. 21
		1802
Francois Aucoin	House, 36' x 22', with gal'y., posts in ground, covered with pickets	
Joseph de Leon	House of posts in ground	Feb. 3
Francois Marie Duhon	House, 26' x 16', on blocks, two gal's. covered with pickets	Mar. 8
Antonio Rodriguez	House, 25' x 15', posts in ground, covered with pickets	June 22
Jean Baptiste Lessard	House, 33' x 16', on blocks, two gal's.	Aug. 14
Pierre Pannevel	House, 20' x 16'	Sept. 11

Settler	Home	Date
		1803
Rafael Croquer	House, 42' x 16'	Jan. 10
Aman Babin	House, 33' x 13', covered with pickets	Mar. 2
Pierre Robro Duplessis	An old cabin	Apr. 29
Pierre Duplessis	House, 30' x 15', 2 gal's.	May 30
Gregoire Dugas	New house, 30' x 18'	June 30
Firmin Blanchard	House, 30' x 16', front and rear gal's.	Sept. 28
Simon Pierre Savoie	House, 26' x 16', built on blocks, 2 gal's.	Oct. 12
Manuel Millien	House, 29' x 12', posts in ground	Nov. 29
		1804
Francois Dugas	House, 45' x 18', two galleries	Feb. 6
Enselm Landry	House, 30' x 10', two gal's., kitchen of posts in ground	Feb. 14
Michel Judice	Semi-double house, 35' x 40', brick chimney, 5 apartments	Mar. 5
Jacob Bobbs	House, 26' x 10', 2 galleries	Mar. 27
Simon Richard	House, 30' x 16', surrounded with pickets, covered with boards	Mar. 20
Joseph Le Blanc	House, 24' x 16', covered with pickets	Apr. 28
Domingo Cabellero	House, 22' x 15'	Dec. 11
Pierre L'Eglise	House, 35' x 41', brick chimney	Dec. 13

Old John A. Marchand Home, Prairieville, La. built about 1870.

On banks of New River about 1921.

The Exiles Build Roads And Levees

F ROM the days of the pioneers to the present time, the cost of building highways and levees has been a heavy burden upon the shoulders of those who dwell upon the banks of the Father of Waters. When the exiles from Acadia settled in the First and Second Acadian coasts, the waters of the old Mississippi, each year at flood-time, flowed freely over the swamps and lowlands of what is now southern Louisiana. No dikes, levees or embankments restrained the progress of the torrents when the waters arose above the banks of the river. It was, therefore, apparent to the first settlers that if they desired to plant, grow and save their crops, it was encumbent upon them to build dikes or leves. The Acadians were poor, and the burden of constructing the levees was indeed a heavy one. In addition to levees, the settlers had to construct a dirt road up and down the Mississippi. Failing to build a levee and a road in front of the lands granted them, the property reverted to the Spanish government or was transferred to another.

As early as April 30, 1770, we find Marie Martha Le Blanc, widow of Jacque Le Chance, declared her inability to construct and maintain the "chemin Royaux"—Royal Road—. She transferred and abandoned her grant of land to one Jeansomme. Later—on Oct. 5, 1780—the congregation of Ascension Catholic church at Lafourche des Chetimaches (now Donaldsonville, La.) concluded that the cost of maintaining the road, levee, ditches and bridges in front of a portion of their land—3 x 40 arpents—was "too heavy a charge on the parishioners," and that the tract should be sold to the highest bidder. Again, on October 9, 1790, Pierre Le Conte declared that he received a grant of land from the Spanish governor; that he could not maintain the levee and the Royal road, and, for these reasons, he abandoned the land to Joseph Babin. Some of the settlers, however, constructed small embankments which they dignified by the term "levees." Thus, on July 23, 1791, Nil Nacdono sold his land to Michel Debergue and described it as having a levee and a "chemin Royaux." On March 29, 1792, however, Joseph Richard and his wife, Cecile Dupuis, declare that they could not maintain the road and levee in front of their grant. Isaac LeBlanc, on March 22, 1794, describes his property as having a "bonne levee." Thus, the years, the seasons and the floods came and passed, and the Acadian exile pursued relentlessly his fight to overcome all obstacles of his day and time.

It appears that the first levee constructed in the lower Mississippi valley was built under the direction of De La Tour, the engineer who,

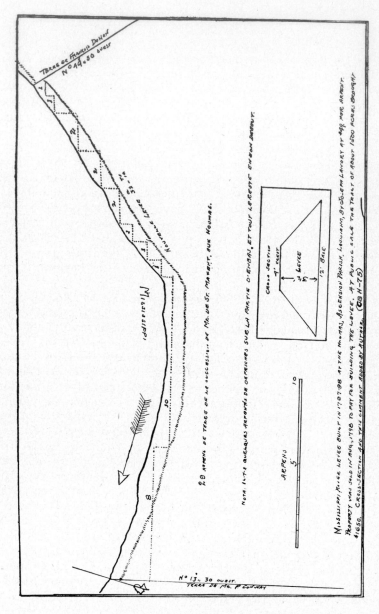

Levee on the Mississippi River at "The Houmas" built by Joseph Landry, in 1797, at $49.00 per arpent.

94

in 1717, planned the city of New Orleans. His plans called for an embankment in front of the future Crescent City. After ten years had expired, Governor Perrier announced that the levee in front of New Orleans had been completed, and he further promised that within a year the levee should be completed for a distance of eighteen miles above and below the city. (Lyle Saxon, "Father Mississippi," p. 257). By 1735, states DuPratz, the levees extended for thirty miles above the city of New Orleans.

The Acadian exiles began arriving as early as 1765, and, in view of the foregoing observations, it appears safe to assume that at the time they settled in the First and Second Acadian settlesment—St. James and Ascension parishes—the lands granted to them were not protected from overflow by levees or dikes. Accordingly, when Governor O'Reilly assumed conrol, he promulgated regulations governing the issuance of land-grants, which regulations are dated February 8, 1770. Under the provisions of these regulations, the settler obligated himself to build, within three years, a levee and road along the Mississippi River in front of the property granted. The settler was also obligated to construct ditches, build bridges and to enclose and clear the front portion of his grant to a depth of two arpents. (Martin, p. 213).

The same historian is authority for the statement that "According to an arrangement between the courts of France and Spain the province (Louisiana) received this year (1785) a very considerable accession of population, by the arrival of a number of Acadian families, who were supported by the French king, and came over to join their friends who had migrated to both sides of the Mississippi river, near Plaquemine; but a number of the families went to increase the settlement . . . on the bayou Lafourche. (Martin, Hist. of La., p. 213).

Birth, marriage, and death records of Ascension Catholic church at Donaldsonville, La., support this statement. The census of 1785 gives the First Acadian settlement (St. James parish) a population of 1332; the Second Acadian settlement (Ascension parish), 646. At Galveston (now Galvez, La.) we find 242, nearly all of who are Spanish settlers. By 1788, the population had increased as follows: St. James, 1559; Lafourche settlement (Ascension parish), 1164, and Galveztown, 268. Judge Martin attributes this large increase in population to the arrival of the Acadians who settled here about 1785. He estimates that at least 3500 had reached Louisiana. The commandant of each district, in addition to being a judge, notary and auctioneer, acted as a road and levee inspector, to see that each settler complied with his obligations to build a road, levee, ditches, bridges, etc. Aside from the fear of the "checking-up" by the commandant, self-preservation demanded and required that the settler erect dirt embankments of some kind to protect crops from overflow. In old Acadia, we are told by Longfellow, the Acadian farms were protected from floods by "Dikes, that the hands of the farmers had raised with labor incessant . . ."

In the archives of the clerk and recorder of the parish of Ascension is found a detailed account—a proces verbal—of the letting of a contract to build a road and levee in front of the property of the succession of Gilbert Antoine de St. Maxent, at the Houmas. Pierre Marigny and Jacques Carrick, syndics, had called the matter to the attention of Evan Jones, commandant of the district. In compliance with the requirements of the law, Evan Jones, on Nov. 5, 1797, went to the front door of the parochial church of Ascension after High Mass, and publicly announced that the contract for the building of a road and levee in front of the property of Gilbert Antoine de St. Maxent, at the Houmas, would be adjudicated to the lowest bidder; that the property and a frontage of 29 or 30 arpents; that the proposed levee must be $\frac{3}{4}$ of an arpent—(192 ft.) from the water's edge; that it must have a 12 ft. base, a 4 ft. crest and a height of $3\frac{1}{2}$ ft. A "huge contract" was about to be awarded to some "lucky" bidder. Jean Baptiste Cazebou, auctioneer, proudly took the rostrum in front of church as soon as the parishioners were dismissed from religious services. He explained what a golden opportunity for profit the levee contract offered. Commandant Evan Jones was at his side, and a large number of citizens stood before him. Raymond Braud, a prominent citizen of the time, opened the bidding. He offered to build the levee, road and necessary ditches and bridges for $75. per arpent—192 ft. Joseph Landry—father of Lieutenant Governor Trasimond Landry—bid $60. per arpent. No adjudication was made, and the sale was postponed two weeks—to Nov. 19, 1797. On the latter date, after High Mass, Auctioneer Cazebou again mounted the rostrum. Joseph Landry repeated his bid of $60. per arpent; Raymond Braud underbid him at $58; Landry went down to $55.; Joseph Melancon surprised the others with a bid of $54. No contract was awarded that day, and the matter was deferred to Sunday, Nov. 26, 1797. After High Mass on that date, Joseph Melancon repeated his bid of $54. per arpent; Joseph Landry submitted a bid of $52.; Raymond Braud, $50., and then Joseph Landry proposed to do the work for $49. per arpent. This bid evidently was a "knock-out" to the others, for Auctioneer Cazebou states that he waited for more than two hours seeking other bidders, and none came forward. The contract was awarded to Joseph Landry (later the first commandant of the American government). Landry obligated himself to execute the work faithfully and exactly as required "before the high water of the coming year." (Orig. Acts "A"-75).

The contractor evidently lost no time in completing the job which he had undertaken, for, on March 7, 1798, Charles Lincour and Paul Landry, syndics of the District of Lafourche des Chetimaches, acting under orders of Commandant Evan Jones, went to the "Houmas" to examine and inspect the road, levee, ditches and bridges built by Joseph Landry, and found that Landry had completed the work "much better than required." On March 5, 1798, Commandant

Jones in person went to inspect the work, and he, like the syndics, reported that everything was done even better than required by the specifications. He measured the levee and found it to be 32 arpents 10 toises. He thereupon prepared the following bill:

32 arpents levee, road, bridges at $49		$1,568.00
plus costs, as follows:		
3 auctions at $5.00	15.00	
3 notices	3.00	
Act of adjudication	3.00	
Copy of act	2.00	
Jean Baptiste Cazebou, auctioneer	2.00	
Land measures or surveyors	16.00	
Plan and copy	3.00	
Total		44.00
Grand total		$1,612.00

Preparing the bill was an easy matter; collecting it was an entirely different proposition. It appears that the succession of Gilbert Antoine de St. Maxent could not pay the foregoing. Accordingly, on August 12, 1798, Commandant Evan Jones went to the front door of Ascension Catholic church and offered the property for sale at public auction. The land was about to be sold to defray the expenses of building the levee, roads, bridges and ditches in front of the property. The property is described as being at the "Houmas", bounded above by Francois Duhon, below by Patrick Conway, with a frontage on the river of 29 arpents and a depth of 40 arpents, the lines opening towards the rear. Joseph Landry and Raymond Braud, leading citizens and competitors in the levee-building matter, again met on the "field of battle." When Commandant Jones called for bids, Joseph Landry offered $1,100 for the property, including levee, road, bridges, etc. Raymond Braud countered with an offer of $1,150; Landry raised his bid to $1,200; Braud then bid $1,300; Paul Landry offered $1,400; Raymond Braud bid $1,500; Landry bid 1,550; Braud increased his bid to $1,600; Landry went to $1,625; and here we note a bid by Louis Faure in the sum of $1,650. This bid was accepted; Mr. Faure paid the $1,650 in cash, and the property—at least 1,500 acres of alluvial land—was formally sold to Louis Faure for about the cost of the levee, road, bridges and ditches. In this connection, the reader may examine 5 Mart. O. E. 459, in reference to a plantation levee in Ascension parish, La. St. Maxent is mentioned in 1 Mart. O. S. 231; 4 Mart. O. S. 621. All of Donaldson Town south of Claiborne street was sold by the sheriff to pay the cost of building a levee on Bayou Lafourche (8 Mart. N. S. 175; 1 La. 137).

Commandant Jones, with the "cash in hand," was now ready to settle the affairs of the succession of the late Gilbert Antoine de St.

Maxent. From the $1,650. received from the sale of the property, he paid to Joseph Landry the amount due him for building the levee, road, etc., $1,612., and from the remainder he paid the costs and expense of the sale of the property. The levee was now built, but the property had "vanished" from the Maxent succession.

A map of this levee is reproduced herein. Whether the tract is situated on the east or west bank of the Mississippi river is somewhat difficult to determine, but, it appears from the arrow that it is situated on the left or east bank near what is now the Riverton plantation, at Burnside, La. The section around Burnside, La., was called "Houmas" in olden days, whereas on the opposite side of the Mississippi, the region is called "Point Houmas."

"Point Houmas" is now owned by Dubourg Thibaut, while "The Houmas," on the opposite bank of the river is owned partly by Remy, Octave, Rene and Clovis Robert, and in part by Edgar J., Wallis, George and Octave Waguespack, all leading planters of that section.

More than one hundred fifty years have rolled into eternity since the Acadian exiles first set foot on the banks of the Father of Waters in the First and Second Acadian settlements, but their descendants still pay heavy tribute to protect their firesides from overflow. It will probably continue so for years upon years—as long as the river flows towards the sea, and in doing so, washes away its sandy banks.

THE FIRST TOWN IN THE SECOND ACADIAN
SETTLEMENT

LET us pause to obtain a bird's-eye view of the Second Acadian settlement as of 1806. We find that Thomas Jefferson is president of the United States of America, and that William C. C. Claiborne is governor of the Territory of Orleans—the present state of Louisiana. The First and Second Acadian settlements (St. James and Ascension parishes, respectively), form the county of Acadia.

A few of the exiles have become prosperous planters, though many of them—in the face of adversities—have made little progress along the road to prosperity. A tribe of Houmas Indians, poor and harmless, dwell a few miles below the Lafourche des Chetimaches on and about Point Houmas; a stage line, making weekly trips over the dirt roads meandering along the Mississippi river, operates between New Orleans and Manchac church—St. Gabriel, La. Two days are required for the trip, and passengers are charged $11. each; a line of so-called "levees" about 5 ft. in height along the Mississippi River afford some protection to the planters from overflow; no steamboat has ever descended the Father of Waters; no post office is found in the whole Acadian settlement; two small newspapers are published in the town of New Orleans; flatboats, pirogues, houseboats and keel-boats transport people and commodities via the Mississippi to New Orleans; and our people daily watch with interest the passing of strange watercraft from the western waters.

Up and down both banks of the Mississippi, through the First and Second Acadian settlements, we find some five hundred families, comprised of the exiles and their descendants. Both settlements contain 2728 white inhabitants and some 2500 slaves, the latter fact indicating that some of the planters are comparatively wealthy. By reason of this wealth some have chosen to refer to these settlements as the "Golden Coast." In addition to the settlers who have established themselves along the Mississippi, we find that a considerable number have established themselves along both banks of Bayou Lafourche. Settlers at the Attakapas and Opelousas have constructed a road along the canal—which is in the rear portion of Napoleonville, La., running from Bayou Lafourche to Lake Verret, and use the canal and road to transport their cattle to the market in New Orleans. (See 4 Mart. O. S. 129). Railroads, electricity, motor vehicles, telephones, radios and a score of other conveniences of the present day were unknown to the settlers.

99

No town or hamlet exists in the whole of the First and Second Acadian settlements. William Donaldson, merchant and bank-director of New Orleans, dreamed of the city that must some day stand at the junction of the Mississippi river and Lafourche des Chetimaches. The ideal spot was just below the entrance to Bayou Lafourche, and this site had been granted by the Spanish governor in 1775 to Pierre Landry, dit Pitre, an Acadian exile. Landry died leaving his widow, Marguerite Allain, and a son, Allain, and probably other children. On the Landry farm we note a dwelling house of 36' x 18', standing on brick pillars, 6',—the levees were about five feet in height—with front and rear galleries; a store building, 22' x 12', with front and rear galleries; a kitchen, 20' x 12', with front and rear galleries; a pigeon house, negro cabin and 40 arpents of land under fence. It appears that the house was situated at what is now the southeast corner of the intersection of Iberville and Houmas Streets, now the home of Marcel Bloch. Widow Marguerite Allain Landry acquired same at the succession sale of her late husband's estate. Donaldson offered her $12,-000 in Mexican gold for the tract, Mrs. Landry to reserve two lots on the second street of the proposed townsite. The offer was accepted, and the act of sale was executed on Monday, February 10, 1806. Within 90 days thereafter—Apr. 27, 1806—Donaldson appeared before his father-in-law, B. F. Van Pradelles, a Notary Public, of New Orleans, and formally dedicated the Ville de Donaldson. (A certified copy of the plat of the original Ville de Donaldson is on file in the Recorder's office of the parish of Ascension, La.). We find that Donaldson named the streets and public places of his new town as follows: Streets—Mississippi, Iberville, Attakapas, Opelousas, Claiborne, Orleans, Pointe Coupee, Concordia, Rapides, Natchitoches, Lafourche, Chetimaches, Houmas, Cabahanosse; public places as follows: Cresent, Louisiana, Acadia, Paragon.

Having acquired a site, Donaldson's next job, of course, was to build his town or city. Naturally many of his friends ridiculed his plans, and laughed at his efforts. But while these friends were pouring "cold water" on the proposition, Donaldson braced-up and inserted the following advertisement in "The Louisiana Gazette," New Orleans, of June 27, 1806:

"Fourche, 21st June, 1806.

"The subscriber begs leave to inform the public that on Monday, the 7th July he shall commence the sale of lots in the town of Donaldson, now establishing at the entrance of the Fourche.

"The plan of the town may be seen at his house on the premises and at his *residence* in New Orleans, where the price and conditions of sale will be made known.

WM. DONALDSON."

The lower boundary line of the original town of Donaldson is approximately 128 ft. east of the eastern side of Cabahanosse street—now Railroad avenue.

The great majority of the first lots sold by Donaldson were along Lafourche street and at "La Pointe"—the intersection of Lafourche and Mississippi streets.

At this time, 1806, no court house or jail existed in all Acadia. (The first session of the county court of Acadia county was held on July 8, 1805, in the Presbytery of the St. James Catholic church, opposite Convent, La. with Michel Cantrelle, judge, presiding.— (Court records, 1805-1839, St. James parish, Convent, La.) It does not appear

"The J. A. Dalferes" building, Mississippi Street near R. R. Ave. now stands at upper boundary line of lands owned by Ascension Catholic church in 1772.

clear where persons charged with offenses or run-away slaves were imprisoned during the French and Spanish regimes; probably at New Orleans. Under the act of the Territorial Legislature of 1805, the justices of the peace of each county were obligated to meet to select parish sites, and devise ways and means of constructing a town hall, jail, etc. On May 27, 1805, Michel Cantrelle, commandant of St. James parish, who was designated by Governor Claiborne as Judge of the county of Acadia, summoned the following named to appear at his residence at Cabahanosse (St. James, La.) for the purpose of receiving their commissions as officials of the county of Acadia, and taking the oaths of office: Hubert Remy, clerk of court; Robert Wederstrandt, sheriff; A. D. Tureau, treasurer; Gaspard Dubuis, Coroner; Louis Mollere, John W. Scott, William Conway, Christophe Colomb, Daniel Blouin, Etienne Reyner, as justice of the peace. Joseph Landry's commission as justice of the peace was sent to him by Mr. Remy.

101

On June 1, 1805, Michel Cantrelle, Hubert Remy, Etienne Reynor, Daniel Blouin, John W. Scott, Christophe Colomb, William Conway, Joseph Landry and Gaspard Dubuys met in convention at the home of Marius Bringier—now Hermitage plantation, Darrow, La.—for the purpose of formulating ways and means of building a court house and jail. When it was proposed to raise $5,000 with which to build a court house and jail, the officials were reminded that the last crop had been almost a total failure. No decision was reached that day, but we find that on September 14, 1806, William Donaldson entered into an agreement with Joseph Landry, Christophe Colomb and Gaspard Dubuys, J. P., obligating himself to build a town hall and prison on lots 48 and 49, at the corner of Attakapas and Chetimaches Streets —at the south-west corner of the intersection of (now) Nicholls Ave. and Chetimaches. This site is now occupied by the law offices of Mayor George R. Blum and Sam A. Le Blanc, Jr., and was formerly occupied by Caleb Cushing Weber as his law office.

Looking backwards after the lapse of a century and a quarter, it appears that Donaldson proposed to the justices of the peace: "Select the ville de Donaldson as the seat of Acadia county, and I will build a town hall and jail at my expense." Donaldson was struggling to develop his town, and money was necessary. Of him, as a bank director, a critic says that he was never absent from a meeting of the board "when his own paper has to pass." He is referred to as "the youthful Donaldson," in January, 1808. By June 17, 1808, his efforts to secure a post-office for his town were successful, and such an office was established "near" the town. At that time it was the only post-office on the Mississippi for a distance of 190 miles above New Orleans. Thomas Randall was appointed first-postmaster. He died shortly after his appointment. His tomb still stands in the Catholic cemetery at Donaldsonville, La.

The infant village has a post-office, but what of the mails? The "Louisiana Gazette," New Orleans, of Nov. 8, 1808, informs us that:

> "The Natchitoches mail, via Lafourche, Opelousas, Attakapas and Rapides, will close on Monday next, the 14th of November, with the Fort Adams mail, and will continue to close with the same mail every other Monday.
> "B. Cenas, P.M."

Thus, we find that the New Orleans mail arrives at Donaldson Town every other Monday. The mails were probably transported by pirogue or other watercraft, or perhaps by some stage line. The exact location of the site of the first post-office is unknown. Governor Claiborne refers to it as "near" the town of Donaldson. Notwithstanding the efforts of Donaldson to advertise his town, it appears to have been unknown to the river folks in general, for in 1809, when the post-office was only one year old, the name was changed to "Lafourche." Perhaps the location of the office was changed when a new post-master was appointed to succeed Thomas Randall, who died in 1808. The location of "La Fourche" post-office was probably beyond the limits of the town of Donaldson. All the settlers for miles up and down the river, as well as all those who operated flat-boats, pirogues, etc., knew where Bayou Lafourche was. William Donaldson, it is sad to relate, did not live to see his name again adorn the post-office building at Donaldson Town.

It appears, however, that Donaldson was fairly successful in disposing of his lots, for—in 1809—we find William Conway, who owned the tract between the Pierre Landry farm and the Catholic church, advertising in "The Gazette," New Orleans, as follows:

> "For Sale. A number of lots adjoining the town of Donaldson; the purchase money will not be required as long as an interest at six per cent per annum is regularly paid; for further particulars apply to Mr. R. (Raymond) Braud residing near the said town, or to the subscriber at his plantation at the Houmas, Sept. 5."

It is noted hereinafter, however, that as late as 1812 Donaldson had sold only two lots on Cabahanosse St.—now Railroad avenue.

The year 1810 found Ascension parish with a population of 2219, of which 1078 were slaves. In September, 1810, Donaldson donated to the county of Acadia (St. James and Ascension parishes) the square bounded by Chetimaches, Opelousas, Attakapas (Nicholls avenue) and Cabahanosse streets. From 1810 continuously and uninterruptedly to this date the Ascension parish court house and jail have stood upon this square. A few miles below the village of Donaldson, in 1810, are about eighty-old Houmas Indians, the remnants of a former mighty tribe.

In February, 1812, Judge Carlier D'Outremer and Wm. S. Watkins wrote William Donaldson—then apparently residing in New Orleans . . . advising him of their desire to construct a drainage ditch along the eastern boundary of the town. On March 2, 1812, Donaldson replied that he had no objection, but referred them to his agent on the premises, Stephen A. Hopkins, attorney. The act granting this 3 ft. strip for a canal or ditch was duly signed by Hopkins, Widow Villeneuve (Lessard), who owned the Lessard tract, Pierre Lafon and Thos. Kennedy. The latter two joined in the act as they owned lots 72 and 73, forming the NE corner of the intersection of Railroad avenue and Iberville street (C.B. 1, fo. 279). This canal ran parallel with Railroad avenue, and it was 128 ft. east of the avenue.

News that the Legislature of the state of Louisiana had, on March 25, 1813, granted a charter to the Ville de Donaldson, was the occasion for great rejoicing on the part of the inhabitants of the village. Donaldson thus became one of the first villages in the state to be chartered as a municipality. The state of Louisiana had been admitted to the Union but a few months. On June 12, 1938 the

"125th Anniversary" of the town was held. The date—June 12th—was selected merely for convenience.

While William Donaldson was in the midst of his labors, striving and struggling to upbuild his fair Ville de Donaldson, the Angel of Death summoned him to his reward. He departed this life at New Orleans, on November 27, 1813, when his incorporated city was only eight months of age. From what church his funeral services were held, and where his mortal remains were laid to rest are unknown to the writer. During the summer of 1813 he realized that the end was approaching, and on August 28th, 1813, he executed his last will and testament before Edward Livingston, New Orleans attorney. It appears that he left no descendants, and his entire estate was bequeathed to his widow, Colgate Van Pradelles. His succession was opened in New Orleans, his legal domicile, at the time of his death.

His widow subsequently married William Moore, of Liberty, Texas. On November 14, 1840, as the wife of Moore, she granted a power of attorney to Albert G. Van Pradelles, authorizing him to handle her business in Louisiana, and particularly in the town of Donaldson. (C.B. 16, fo. 362). Van Pradelles, on January 22, 1841, sold to the trustees of the town of Donaldson, represented by Andrew Gingry, president of the Board, all the batture in front of said town, also all public places, the Crescent and all the ground belonging originally to William Donaldson within the said town, contained in Donaldson's title and not divided into lots, "except the lot claimed by the Freemasons," for a cash consideration of $1,000. (C.B. 16, fo. 368).

Thus, after the expiration of thirty-five years, we find the family of William Donaldson severing forever their connection with the city which he established at the Lafourche des Chetimaches.

FAUBOURG LESSARD.

We have seen from the foregoing that the original town of Donaldson was established on the Pierre Landry farm. Immediately below the Landry tract, is situated what was in olden times the farm of Jean Baptiste Lessard, dit Villeneuve, with a frontage on the Mississippi River of one arpent, one toise. The Lessard tract is the upper portion of the tract purchased by Etienne Landry from the Congregation of the Ascension Catholic church in October, 1780, for the sum of $242. By 1805, the upper portion of the Etienne Landry tract had been acquired by Lessard, who subdivided it into lots under the name of "Faubourg Lessard." Widow Lessard, nee Marie Lorote Villeneuve, began selling lots in her subdivision in 1812-18. In the course of time, keen rivalry developed between Donaldson Town, on the one hand, and Faubourgs Lessard and Conway, on the other. Donaldson Town was making steady progress, for, in 1816, William Darby, an early writer, states that the "thriving town of Donaldsonville . . . is the first village on the Mississippi above New Orleans worth notice."

Under the charter of March 25, 1813, the boundary of the town is

104

declared to be "the land laid off into lots by William Donaldson," but under the charter of March 7, 1823, the lower boundary of the town is fixed as the "land formerly belonging to Md. Villeneuve." It appears that the upper boundary line of the Lessard tract was a point 128 ft. east of Railroad avenue, while the lower line was Lessard street.

FAUBOURG CONWAY.

Immediately below the Lessard, dit Villeneuve, tract came the farm of William Conway, who appears to have resided on Conway plantation, now Burnside, La. This is the lower portion of the land which was purchased by Etienne Landry from the Catholic congregation in October, 1780, and it extended to what is now St. Patrick street. Conway was a native of Ireland, and naturally the name "St. Patrick" must not be omitted. It is found that William Conway, as early as 1809, advertised lots for sale in "Faubourg Conway," as follows:

"For sale. A number of lots adjoining the town of Donaldson; the purchase money will not be required as long as an interest of six per cent. per annum is regularly paid; for further particulars apply to Mr. R (aymond) Braud residing near the said town, or to the subscriber at his plantation at the Houmas. Sept. 5, 1809) ."

It is interesting to note that William Donaldson also sold lots on the "pay interest only" plan. His widow tried to collect, and had considerable difficulty. (1 La. 29) .

By 1840, Faubourgs Lessard and Conway had acquired a considerable population, and the inhabitants thereof were incorporated into a municipality. For some unknown reason the two faubourgs were not annexed to the already incorporated town of Donaldson. They were incorporated as "Unionville" by Act 83 of 1840, and had a mayor and five aldermen. (See, also Act 12 of 1843; Act 95 of 1840) . However, it appears that an understanding was reached within a few years for, by the Act of Apr. 22, 1846, Unionville was merged into Donaldsonville. (See, batture case, 11 La. 140, Conway heirs) .

The size of the town was reduced by the charter of 1823. William Donaldson died in 1813, and in 1816 all that portion of the town situated in the rear (south) of Claiborne street was sold by the sheriff to pay the cost of constructing a levee on Bayou Lafourche in front of this tract of land. Gabriel Winter, at the public sale, became the purchaser at $680. The land was entirely in woods at the time. Winter enclosed the whole tract, and later transferred it to R. R. Barrow. It appears that the latter caused it to be subdivided into "Winter's lots." In the charter of 1823 the southern boundary line of the town was fixed as "the property of Gabriel Winter." Winter objected to his land being taxed by the municipal authorities. The supreme court decided that his land was outside of the town. (See

8 Mart. N. S. 553; 24 Ann. 342; C. B. 18, fo. 88, 359; C. B. 28, fo. 576; 23 Ann. 342).

CHURCH LAND BETWEEN ST. PATRICK AND ST. VINCENT STREETS.

Immediately below St. Patrick street, and extending to St. Vincent street, is a body of land (excluding that of St. Vincent's Institute) which was owned by the Catholic church until some fifty-five years ago. Many of the old residents here remember the time when those having dwelling houses on this tract paid "ground rent" to the church. Such was the case when Father Ceuppens began work on the church of 1775. However, some forty-odd years ago the land was subdivided by P. D'Hemecourt, surveyor, and from time to time the church sold lots to the inhabitants. That portion of the church tract situated in the rear of the Texas & Pacific Railway is known to this day as "Churchville." Below St. Vincent street, and extending to the lower line of the church property—about 100 ft. west of Church street—is situated the tract of land whereon stands the magnificent church edifice which took so many years to build, and which to-day is among the most beautiful churches in the state. The Presbytery, Catholic High school for boys, and the present Catholic cemetery are all situated on this tract of land. It appears that it has been so used continuously from 1772 to the present time.

PEYTAVIN PLANTATION

Immediately below the church land is found "old Peytavin" plantation, owned in the old days by Antoine Peytavin, the contractor who built the state house in Donaldsonville, 1825-1830. The upper portion of Peytavin was subdivided about 1910, under the name of "Lemann Addition." The Donaldsonville High School, and a large number of modern residences have been erected here.

THE SECOND TOWN IN THE SECOND ACADIAN SETTLEMENT

Exactly one hundred years subsequent to the founding of the ville de Donaldson by William Donaldson, the town of Gonzales was founded and established by Joseph Gonzales. About the year 1906, Mr. Gonzales subdivided portions of the west half of the northwest quarter of section twenty-eight, and the east half of the northeast quarter of section twenty-nine, township nine south, range three east, into town lots. However, a post-office bearing that name was established at the site of the town many years prior to 1906. From the days of his young manhood, Joseph Gonzales had visions of a town that would some day arise on the spot, and would serve the entire eastern portion of Ascension parish. During the years 1903-08 the Louisiana Railway & Navigation Co. built its line running from Shreveport to New Orleans, and Joseph Gonzales decided that the hour to sub-divide portions of his lands into town lots had arrived.

Mr. Gonzales was born at St. Amant, La., about the year 1862, the son of Joseph Gonzales, Sr. (Civil War sheriff) and Adorea Marchand. In his youth, educational facilities in the New River section were very limited, and Joseph Gonzales, by reason of that fact, acquired only a grammar school education. At an early age he entered the commercial field. As early as 1883 he was a clerk in the store of John Crosley's Sons (an English concern), on Southwood plantation, about one mile above Geismar, La., where the writer's late father, John Alcide Marchand, Sr., also worked. A few years thereafter he formed a co-partnership with his brother, Alexander F. Gonzales, and they established a small retail store in the old "Paul Landry" store building, on the south bank of New River, about 1200 ft. above Burnside street, where the town of Gonzales now stands. In those days, the settlers lived far apart, a one-room school building was found here and there, mail was carried semi weekly on horse back from New River post-office (now Geismar, La.) by Solomon Barman, father of Chief Deputy Clerk of Court James S. Barman; a dirt road, which became in horrible condition at each rainy spell, meandered along New River bayou from Moore's bridge to the lower reaches of the New River settlement, now Acy, La.; electric lights, automobiles, telephones, radios, paved roads, graveled roads, gas and modern school buildings were things uninvented and unheard of. A post-office had been established at the present site of Gonzales, La., after the Civil War under the name of "White Houmas," with Vincent Adlard Landry as first post-master, but this office was discontinued on Apr. 3, 1877.

In his little store on New River during the years 1886 and 1887 Joseph Gonzales discussed with the pioneers the great need for a post-office at Gonzales. In our mind's eye we can see him waving his arms and gesticulating in a presentation of the matter to settlers like Jean Nargassans, J. D. (Minet) Elisar, Leon Gautreau, Abe Wright, Henry Parker, Ulger "Shoon" Bourque, Velior Bourque, Charles Gaudin, Louis Gaudin, C. Narcisse Gautreau, John A. Marchand, Sr. (father of the writer), Allen W. Martin, father of Dr. D. T. Martin, Fred. Gonzales, father of Sheriff Lester Gonzales, Solomon Barman, early mail carrier, John M. Lusk, justice of the peace, Dr. P. T. St. Amant, father of C. V. St. Amant, Cleophas (Toots Bourque, Lucien Gautreau, Stanville Le Blanc, Alexis Le Blanc, Lee Hamilton, M. Beauregard Gautreau, John Mire, father of Vic P. Mire, former sheriff, Vincent T. Landry, brother-in-law of Lester E. Wright, Paul Landry, Theogene (Choke) Braud, C. Daniel Blouin, Leon Duplessis, father of L. B. (Capt.) Duplessis, Dorcini Dubois, Gille Gautreau, Adolph Braud, Adolph (Mastock) Blouin, Bill Braud, and a host of other early settlers. Mr. Gonzales believed in petitions, and he probably obtained the signatures of a great many of the above named to a petition addressed to the post-office department praying for the establishment of the post-office at Gonzales, La. Even his political enemies conceded that he was a tireless worker, and he was determined to secure a post-office. There were post-offices at New River lane, Dutchtown, Galvez, Hope Villa, Prairieville and St. Amant, but none where the progressive town of Gonzales now stands. The untiring efforts of Mr. Gonzales were rewarded with success, and on May 21, 1887, Gonzales post-office was established with Joseph Gonzales as first postmaster.

At that time no road ran from Burnside to Gonzales. The writer recalls distinctly that a trip from Gonzales to Burnside about the year 1900 involved using a winding trail through the lowlands between Carencro and the rear of Burnside plantations. Many of the older residents will recall that, as late as twenty-five years ago, it was necessary to open and close three plantation gates to reach Burnside from Gonzales.

When the L. R. & N. Co. built its line (now the L. & A.) they located the station at a point about one-fourth mile above its present location, and named it "Edenborn"—in honor of Wm. Edenborn, owner of the railroad line. Joseph Gonzales led the fight to compel the L. R. & N. to move its station to a point south of New River bayou, and to change the name to Gonzales, so as to conform to the name of the post-office. After a contest lasting several years, the L. R. & N. was ordered to make the desired change.

In 1922 the town was incorporated as a municipality, and Joseph Gonzales was commissioned as its first mayor. He served in this capacity for many years. Prof. Harrison Young succeeded him, and the latter was succeeded by J. Paul Bourgeois, contractor and publisher, who still pilots the "ship of state" at this writing.

Joseph Gonzales, the founder and father of the town of Gonzales, was indeed a tireless worker. Day in and day out he struggled to upbuild the New River country. As a friend of schools, churches, roads, drainage, gas lines, water-works and electricity, he always stood in the foremost ranks. He was married but once and then to Felicite Bourgeois, aunt of the present mayor. He departed this life on April 20th, 1940, while attending a funeral. His widow and the following children survived him, to-wit: Felicie (Mrs. H. Earl Holliday), Beatrice (Mrs. John W. Tanner), Josephine (Mrs. B. H. Andrews), Fanny, and Ethel (Mrs. Morris E. McKinery). Funeral services were conducted at St. Theresa's Catholic church, at Gonzales, La., with interment in the church cemetery.

Louisiana's State House at Donaldsonville, 1830-31.

Left to right: Staff Sergeant Joseph Yve Landry, Jr., now in England; Lieutenants Roy Francis Sentilles and Sidney Albert Marchand, Jr., now at Fort Dix, N. J.

Index